RED RIVER CITY

A HISTORY OF
NORTHERN NEW MEXICO
1800 - 2000

J. Rush Pierce

JRP Publications
2008

Red River City, A History of Northern New Mexico 1800-2000

Copyright @ J. Rush Pierce, 2008.
 All rights reserved by the author. Any reproduction of any source must have written permission of the author.

JRP Publications
9319 Ravenswood
Granbury, TX 76049
         or
P.O. Box 489
Red River, NM 87558

Designed by Marlene Tyrrell
Printed by Taylor Publishing Co., Dallas, Texas

ISBN 978-0-9707640-2-7

For our sons
Rush, Ben, Frank, Scott

PREFACE

The town of Red River has had a fascinating and varied history. In the beginning it was a gold rush town (a "Gold Camp") which initially prospered and then began to slowly die. At this point the introduction of the automobile and the rise of the summer family vacation brought a transformation and new growth. The spectacular scenic beauty and cool summer climate drew an increasing number of visitors so that by the mid-twentieth century the town was well known as a summer tourist attraction. After World War II, change came again as Red River took on a new identity, becoming a winter ski resort. Today the town can prosper and grow as a year round attraction, and already seems to be on the threshold of further transformation.

In 1995 the town of Red River held its centennial celebration. Over the preceding span of a hundred years a number of writings, essays, memoirs, and books had appeared, denoting various aspects of Red River history. One of the first of these, Winnie Hamilton's *Wagon Days in Red River*, published in 1947, is largely a memoir of events in the lives of her family during the early days. However, it also contains a number of historical facts as well as information about the settlers of the first fifty years. This book served as a model and catalyst for those who came later and were inspired to write their own memoirs. The list includes: Ruth Yeager's *Red River Community House*, a story of how the Community House came into being; Tillie Simeon's *Tillie*, a memoir of the Simeon family; Kenneth Balcomb's *The Red River Hill*, published in 1981 and detailing the building of the Red River Pass Road; and Lester Lewis' *Growing Up in Red River, New Mexico*.

The best historical book concerning Red River is by Jim Berry Pearson, *The Red River - Twining Area: A New Mexico Mining Story*, written in 1986. It is detailed, well researched, and contains many footnotes and references. However, it only covers the early mining

PREFACE

period, up to about 1935, and there is no similar study for the latter half of the century. In short, no complete history of Red River has so far been produced and this fact is a major reason for the production of this book.

At the outset I decided that the book would be based almost entirely upon written sources. This, of course, has the distinct advantage that the information is likely to be more accurate. But there is a downside. If some event, activity, or person has not been recorded or written about, then that individual or happening will be short changed or left out. This is unfortunate but a byproduct of relying on written material. There is the additional problem that the amount of recorded information is somewhat limited since during much of the town's history there was no regular newspaper. However, a review of the Bibliography and Appendix A will show a considerable list of resources. Additionally, I was able to use many of the records of the Red River Historical Society and these proved invaluable.

There is one reminder. For any historical story there needs to be a cut off date. I have arbitrarily chosen to close the book at the year 2000. Events or happenings after this date are not included.

The reciting of historical events can oftentimes become boring so in an effort to enliven the story I have done a couple of things. The numbered "Notes" which are scattered throughout are not footnotes but instead are general notes which expand on and give a lighter side to the text. I would strongly advise the reader to look at these as you go; you will find it rewarding.

In another move to add interest to the text I have intentionally brought into the story as many people and families as possible. This helps to personalize the story and also emphasizes the fact that what we call history is simply the sum total of the histories of individual people. In Appendix A there is a listing of many of the Red River people and families who have played at least some role in the "making" of this history. I hope that this listing along with

PREFACE

the various references may be a source of study and research for future writers and historians.

The illustrations in the book came from several sources. The oldest photos (especially those in Chapter Two) were obtained from the Museum of New Mexico archives. Another source for some of the early pictures is the Aultman Studio in Trinidad. Colorado. Otis Aultman was probably the first photographer to come into this area and he made a number of photographs in the 1890s. Some of his original 8 by 10 inch plate glass negatives are still used for making prints. As one might expect, the great majority of photos came from the large picture collection held by the Red River Historical Society. A small number of illustrations are from my own photographs. You must remember that some of these photos are close to one hundred years old and the quality is not always the best.

I am indebted to the Red River Historical Society which has made the book possible by providing photos and its historical archives. There are a few people who have helped along the way by providing inspiration, guidance, encouragement, and assistance: Winnie Hamilton, Frances Williams, John Brandenburg, Glen Calhoun, Fritz Davis, Lee Romig, Kerry Shepherd, and Bob Prunty among others. As always, Marlene Tyrrell Pierce has done all the layout, photo arrangement, and basic editing and for this I am grateful. And of course, my wife and soul mate, Amanda, has remained patient and helpful during all the time spent in research and writing.

J. Rush Pierce

CONTENTS

Chapter 1 -- PLACE 1
Chapter 2 -- PRELUDE 11
Chapter 3 -- GOLD FEVER 41
Chapter 4 -- RED RIVER CITY 73
Chapter 5 -- TRANSITION 113
Chapter 6 -- YEAR ROUND RESORT 157
Chapter 7 -- INCORPORATION 189
NOTES 207
   Chapter 1 207
   Chapter 2 209
   Chapter 3 215
   Chapter 4 223
   Chapter 5 229
   Chapter 6 235
   Chapter 7 239
APPENDIX A 241
APPENDIX B 247
BIBLIOGRAPHY 248

PLACE

The story of Red River is one of place and people and time. Place mostly, for this is the bedrock upon which any community is founded. It is place, or location, which determines such things as natural resources, climate, access, water, and natural scenery, all of the things which decide whether a given town will become a trading center, farm community, mining town, crossroads or a magnet for tourists. It is, however, a town's people, especially the earliest or founding settlers, who give it flavor and personality, who largely determine whether the community will become vibrant, placid or even stagnant; it is usually the case that most towns take on the character and personality of their people. And then there is time or history, which is fickle, unpredictable, and unyielding. There are always factors beyond the community's borders, forces that are economic, social, cultural, and these can decide a given town's destiny and fate.

The town of Red River was founded on its proximity to precious metals and the strange, almost frenzied, fever for gold and silver. The earliest settlers were miners and prospectors along with those who followed in their wake: merchants, builders, saloon-keepers, and craftsmen plus the usual assortment of speculators, schemers, and deal-makers. For nearly thirty years Red River was essentially a gold mining town and this gave to it a distinctive flavor and personality which is evidenced today in the names of its streets and many of its establishments. On a deeper level, these early miners bestowed upon the community certain traits and characteristics which would help it live on as the gold boom began to fade--an appreciation for hard work, perseverance in the face of adversity, a strong sense of individualism, and an optimistic outlook.

As the ore started to play out, the fever and fervor began to wane and the town of Red River commenced to dwindle. Many of its citizens abandoned the area in search of opportunity elsewhere and it seemed as if the town would suffer the fate of other mining camps, slowly becoming another ghost town. But those left behind slowly turned to the other great assets of the Valley, its remarkable scenic beauty and its cool summer climate. They began to realize the possibilities that could flow from promoting the area as a summer vacation and tourist attraction. So, with hard work, perseverance, and optimism they began to lure visitors to come and enjoy the high mountains, lakes, streams, and cool weather. People from Texas, Oklahoma, Kansas, and elsewhere came in ever increasing numbers and the majority of those who visited returned again and again. The old mining town gave way to a new community and the old personality was replaced by a new one.

The southern Rocky Mountains are split by the San Luis and Rio Grande Valleys into two long mountain chains. The easternmost extension stretches from southern Colorado south to Pecos and separates the Great Plains from the arid intermountain region of northern New Mexico. This range of mountains has long been known by the melodious name of Sangre de Christo.(1) These are rugged mountains which rise up several thousand feet above the prairie, presenting a formidable barrier for those early settlers traveling westward to Santa Fe and Taos. There are only a few passes which penetrate this range and they were hazardous in summer and impassable in winter. The safest and most hospitable route skirted the mountains completely, following along the eastern slopes southward to Las Vegas and Pecos and then turning north to the Spanish settlements. This became the Santa Fe Trail.

In northern New Mexico the Sangre de Christo range is dominated by Wheeler Peak, at 13,161 feet the highest point in the state.

Its close neighbor, Gold Hill at 12,711 feet, is almost as high. The entire region consists of countless canyons, high ridges, and clear snow melt streams. These mountains divide two great watersheds, those streams flowing westward entering the Rio Grande, while those descending east eventually become part of the Mississippi.

As spring comes to the Sangre de Christo mountains snows high on the northeastern face of Wheeler Peak begin to melt, forming small pools, ponds, and trickles. These begin to run downward and are joined by countless other streamlets, seeps and springs. All of this cascading water gains speed and momentum as it plunges two thousand feet to the valley floor to form the beginning of the major branch, or East Fork, of the Red River. The river at this point flows almost due north for about five miles, is joined first by Sawmill Creek, and then reaches a juncture with the Middlefork Creek, the other of the main tributaries. This latter stream has its origin on the northern flank of Wheeler Peak but is also fed by runoff from Fraser Mountain.(2) It cascades down the Middlefork canyon, is joined by the West Fork, then turns eastward for a mile to join the East Fork.

At the juncture of the East Fork and Middlefork the canyon spreads into an open valley which extends northward another three or four miles. This is known today as the Upper Valley and is the site of numerous cabins and homes. Here the Red River receives three more stream tributaries having the rather disparate names of Bear Creek, Black Copper Creek, and Fourth of July Creek. Again the canyon narrows for about three miles and the river is joined by Goose and Placer Creeks.

Not far below Placer, the river begins a turn to the west and the canyon opens into a more broad valley extending about two miles. This is the Red River Valley which became the location of the present-day town of Red River. Along this stretch of the river and now located within the town are three other tributaries, Bitter Creek, Mallette Creek and Pioneer Creek. West of town the river begins

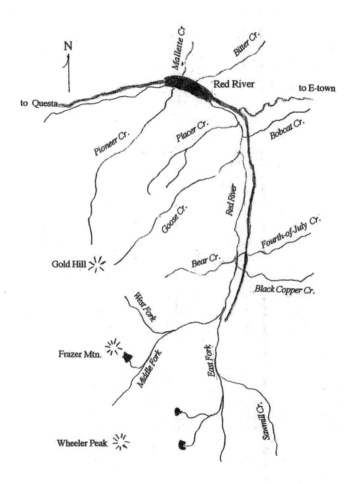

Map of the Red River with its streams and tributaries

to descend through a more narrow canyon, cascading and tumbling for ten miles to the town of Questa. Here there is only a brief pause before it plunges the short distance to empty into the Rio Grande.

Visitors coming to Red River from the east travel through Cimarron, drive up the Cimarron River Canyon and at Eagle Nest enter the Moreno Valley. This scenic valley lies just over the mountain ridge from the Red River valley and was known by the old timers as a "hanging valley". It extends north and south for about thirty miles and is several miles wide. Because of its proximity to Red River, much of the history of these two areas is intertwined. The highway from Eagle Nest travels north up the Moreno Valley, ascends to Bobcat Pass, and then drops a thousand feet into the town of Red River. Today this journey is made in a matter of minutes, but in the days before roads were built it was a long and arduous trip, even on horseback. The western gateway to the Valley is through Questa and the ten miles of winding highway that climbs through the scenic canyon of the Red River. This trip seems quick and pleasant now but in roadless days it required a day's journey with frequent stream crossings. To the north of Red River are valleys extending east and west, separated by high mountain ridges which makes travel in this direction difficult at best. And to the south lies the great massif of Wheeler Peak, Gold Hill, Red Dome, Fraser, and Bull-of-the-Woods. All of this topography makes the Red River Valley isolated and remote even today. In the days of horse and foot travel this remoteness was magnified many fold and accounts for the fact that settlers and miners came late to the area.

The town of Red River lies at an altitude of 8,750 feet, surrounded by densely wooded slopes of the Carson National Forest. Those who come to this area and spend much time here will find themselves passing through several plant life zones as they climb to higher altitude. The trees, shrubs, and flowers will be different depending on the elevation and these floral Life Zones point out the varying plant habitats. There is an interesting aspect to this effect: the deep forests at 10,000 feet resemble the woodlands of northern Montana, while the plant life above timberline is similar to that of the northern Canadian tundra. Thus, a climb in elevation of several thousand feet is equivalent to traveling north several hundred miles. In other words, going up in altitude is the same as going north in latitude.

The Red River Valley is located in the Montane Zone (or mixed conifer zone) which in general extends from 7,500 to 9,000 feet. Here are found fully developed forests of ponderosa pine, lodgepole pine, Douglas fir, and white fir. At the higher levels are Englemann spruce and a few subalpine fir. Deciduous trees in this zone are aspen, scrub oak (Gambel's oak), cottonwood, willow, and alder.

Traveling higher one enters the Subalpine Zone (or spruce-fir woodland zone) at elevations of 9,000 feet to tree line. This zone is characterized by lush, almost "primeval" forests in which are found Englemann spruce, subalpine fir, Douglas fir, limber pine, lodgepole pine, blue spruce, and bristlecone pine. The only deciduous trees of any significance are the aspen.

The Alpine Zone (or alpine tundra zone) is by definition that area found above timberline, which in this region lies above 11,500 feet. Of course there are no trees here, only grasses, sedges, dwarf shrubs, and the tundra flowers. Alpine tundra is rarely found in the vicinity of Red River except near the crests of Wheeler Peak and Gold Hill.

Those coming into or going out of Red River will travel through another lower plant life habitat, the Foothills Zone (or pinon-juniper zone) which is situated between 6,000 and 7,500 feet. In the lower parts of this zone occur pinon pine and juniper, often somewhat widely spaced and accompanied by grasses and shrubs. Higher up begin ponderosa pine and then a few Douglas fir and white fir. Scrub oak, cottonwood, willow, and alder make up the deciduous varieties.(3)

All of these floral zones are found in the vicinity of Red River and can almost be covered in a single day of hiking. This accounts for the wide variety and diversity of plant life in so small an area. The wide range of habitats supports many different types of trees, shrubs, grasses, and wildflowers and also provides a home for a host of animal life. Although most of the area is covered by thick forests, there are any number of meadows which are known as mountain "parks". These can vary in size from a few square feet to many acres and add to the plant and animal diversity.

The high mountain location and altitude account for Red River's climate of cool summers and harsh winters. To the flatland visitors who come to escape the prairie heat of summer, the weather here seems delightful, and it is. Daytime temperatures average 75 degrees while overnights are about 40. Humidity is usually low, ten to twenty per cent, and this can produce wide swings in temperature during a 24 hour cycle. It is not uncommon for an overnight low near freezing to give way to an afternoon of eighty degrees. June through August might be called the true summertime since both May and September often have freezing temperatures and an occasional snow. Winters are both harsh and long, beginning in October and lasting well into April. In winter the average days are about forty degrees with drops at night to near zero. These average figures fail to tell the whole story since record lows can be minus forty and there are occasionally balmy winter days of near sixty.

Annual precipitation, while considerably greater than other parts of New Mexico, is still only just above 20 inches. Roughly half of this is in the form of snow. Heaviest rainfall occurs during July and August, the months of summer "monsoon" rains, when afternoon showers are the rule. Snowfall averages around 140 inches but this is highly variable as to when and where it occurs. There is also considerable variation from year to year, with a high of 301 inches in 1978-79 and only 19 inches in 1949-50. The snow that does fall melts slowly and this recharges the streams, rivers, springs, and aquifers. As a result this region is one of the few in the state which seems to have ample water.(4)

The first great natural resources of the region to be exploited were the mineral assets. Gold was discovered about the time of the Civil War and as a result hundreds of prospectors and miners descended on the area. They wandered over much of the country in search of a rich strike and settled in many of the canyons and valleys; towns appeared--Elizabethtown, Amizette, La Belle, and ultimately Red River. Over more than four decades the search went on but the great bonanza could not be found. Only Baldy Mountain in the Moreno Valley produced great riches.

This region of the Sangre de Christos proved to be a source of several other minerals. Coal was first discovered near Raton around 1880 and mines were operated for a number of years. Later, in the 20th century, an extensive coal mining operation was carried out at Dawson.(5) Copper was found at Twining on the Rio Hondo and for a time was effectively mined. The Moly mine near Questa, opened about 1930 and still in production today, was at one time the richest and second largest molybdenum mine in the world.

Another natural resource, timber, is found in the extensive forests of this area but has not been much exploited. For quite some time most of the area has been under the control of the Carson National Forest so that tree cutting is strictly regulated. There have been times in the past when selective logging has been carried out and there remain old logging roads in the Red River vicinity. In recent years, for a variety of reasons, this type of activity has all but disappeared.

In short, the Red River valley is a place of high rugged mountains, is somewhat remote and difficult of access, blessed with a near perfect summer climate but also with what can be bitter cold during the long months of winter. It is a place of summer mountain showers and heavy winter snows and also is home to dense forests and various mineral resources. But it is much more than this. It is also a place of snow-capped peaks, tumbling streams, clear mountain lakes, and high mountain vistas. A place of verdant forest ridges outlined against cobalt skies, of green mountain meadows splashed with bright wildflower colors, of freshly scented air, and a home to deer, bear, and elk. Much of it is still pristine and it is a place of exceptional natural beauty.

10

PRELUDE
(1820 - 1860)

Look at a map of the Red River valley and take note of the names of the river's tributaries. None of these carries a Spanish name, none is denoted by one of those musical-sounding, almost poetic Spanish words so frequently found throughout New Mexico. Instead, all of the streams bear Anglo-American names: Pioneer, Goose, Sawmill, Bear, Black Copper, Mallette, etc. This illustrates the fact that this area was settled in the very beginning by Americans, there being no indigenous Spanish or Mexican culture in the Valley. The first prospectors, miners, and homesteaders came here from the United States so that from its founding the town of Red River has carried the American stamp.

This is not to imply that Red River escaped the Spanish influence, for it did not and still does not. All of New Mexico has been heir to the influence of Spain (and later, Mexico) and the effect of this continues to shape the life and culture of this particular land. Before the 19th century New Mexico was ruled by Spain for well over two hundred years and the Spanish heritage went down very deeply into the soul and heart of the people. It is evident yet today in such surface expressions as language, dress, cuisine, and social customs. In a more profound way the land inherited certain ideas and customs from Spain having to do with legal and judicial systems, property and water rights, an aristocracy, taxation, the role of government, and the status of the Pueblos. Reflections of these attitudes can still be seen.

Spain was always very jealous of her colonies and frequently employed the Spanish soldiers to carefully and closely guard the frontiers. Outsiders were mistrusted and any who penetrated the borders were either turned away or captured and imprisoned.(1) Trade with Americans or French-Canadians was generally prohibited and any that did occur was strictly regulated. The sanctioned trade routes of New Mexico ran north and south, from the merchants of Chihuahua up the Rio Grande to Santa Fe and Taos. Over time many of the people came to realize how much this was to their disadvantage, since American goods were cheaper and consisted of a much greater variety. However, so long as the Spanish rulers in Mexico City continued the tightly controlled and regulated trade policy, nothing could be done.

As the 19th century opened, momentous change was in the wind.

In 1821 the people of Mexico found victory in their revolution and became independent of Spain. In the northern territory of New Mexico there was little immediate effect except for a complete reversal of the policy in regard to trade. Whereas association and trade with foreigners had been banned under Spanish rule, now the people of Santa Fe and Taos welcomed the American traders and their wealth of goods. Almost immediately the doors were opened and merchandise began to flow westward. The fact that this trade developed so quickly was the result of the large fur trade which had been established in the previous fifteen years.

Following the Louisiana Purchase in 1803 and the subsequent Lewis and Clark expedition, there was widespread awareness and publicity regarding the vast Rocky Mountain region and its resources. As a result hundreds of men were drawn to the mountains, wandering up the many rivers, across countless ranges, and through canyons and valleys. They covered vast distances and were often exposed to great danger. Mostly young, mostly single, they were a motley collection of explorers, adventurers, and trappers and became known as mountain men. Most of them were in search of riches, which were readily found in the fur trade. At the time there was a large, growing, and very lucrative market in beaver pelts, occasioned by the popularity of fashionable beaver hats. The Rockies were filled with beaver and a young man, if hardy and industrious, could accumulate a surprising income from a season of trapping. Soon the word began to spread and in ever-increasing numbers they came, drawn to the western mountains in search of furs. They would set out from the settlements accompanied by pack horses and mules, spend a season or two along the mountain rivers, and then return east with their animals laden with pelts. In towns along the Mississippi or Missouri the goods would be sold and after a time the trappers would set out again.

It was not long before a few of the more enterprising among them realized that money could be made by moving supplies westward to the vicinity of the trappers themselves. Goods were carried by pack horse to a prearranged rendezvous in the mountains and there the merchandise was exchanged for furs which were then brought back by the trader to the eastern towns. This fur trading system proved to be popular as well as profitable and it grew quickly and became highly organized. In this manner the large fur trading companies came into being, each employing large numbers of men. These traders soon were accustomed to moving large amounts of goods through rough and dangerous country under the most adverse conditions.

In the very year of Mexican independence, a Missourian by the name of William Becknell decided to attempt a trading expedition to New Mexico even though it would be a long and hazardous trip. He departed Franklin, Missouri in September of 1821 with pack mules and accompanied by four men. The small group followed the Arkansas River westward through Kansas and into southern Colorado. At the Purgatory they turned southwest to the vicinity of Trinidad and then climbed the Raton Pass into New Mexico. Skirting the mountains, the journey proceeded south to Las Vegas and San Miguel near the Pecos. A short climb over Apache Pass, a turn

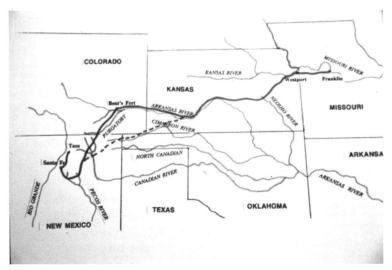
The early Santa Fe Trail

A typical view of the Santa Fe Trail near Ft. Union, NM.
Picture courtesy of the Museum of New Mexico, #12845

Wagons at the Governor's Palace, Santa Fe Plaza--late nineteenth century
Picture courtesy of the Museum of New Mexico, #11264

to the north, and they reached Santa Fe, arriving nearly two months after their departure. The traders were welcomed with open arms and soon disposed of their merchandise. American goods were in great demand because they were cheaper, of better quality, and of more variety than what traditionally came north from the Chihuahua merchants. Becknell and his companions returned to Franklin with a considerable profit.

To Becknell goes the honor and credit for opening the Santa Fe Trail and it soon became a highway. Becknell, himself, returned to Santa Fe the next year and this time he used three wagons to carry his goods. Hoping to avoid the Raton Pass he followed a shortcut across the plains of southwestern Kansas that led directly into New Mexico. This became the famous Cimarron Cutoff which, though dry, and hard on men and animals, was used by many future travelers. By 1824 Becknell was able to organize a large party of 80 men

Typical early Taos street scene, late nineteenth century
Picture courtesy of the Museum of New Mexico, #9649

and 25 wagons. The trip was successful and his investment of $30,000 in merchandise brought a return of $180,000. Reports of his profits lured many to follow in his foot steps, so that within ten years the value of goods carried over the Santa Fe Trail increased over ten fold.(2)

The starting point of the Trail gradually moved westward from Franklin to Independence and then to Westport Landing (in present day Kansas City). From there to Santa Fe was 835 miles by the Mountain Branch (via the Raton Pass) and 780 miles if the Cimarron Cutoff was taken. This distance made it easy to make the trip west and back in a single summer season. The caravans became large and organized with many men and wagons, the latter pulled by mules and later by oxen. Goods were varied: cotton, woolen and silk goods of all kinds; shoes and clothing; notions such as needles,

PRELUDE   17

pins, thread, and buttons; cutlery and utensils; hardware, such as saws, hammers, hoes, and spades. All of these were sold outright or traded for furs and wool. With time it became the practice to transport a portion of the merchandise further south into New Mexico or even as far as Chihuahua.(3)

Early on the Santa Fe Trail was extended north to Taos and it became the western terminus of the trail. This town, located close to the southern Rockies, soon became the center of fur trade in northern New Mexico. It was convenient for trappers to come south out of the mountains to Taos bringing their furs which were traded or sold there and then sent back over the Santa Fe Trail to the eastern settlements. As a result many of the mountain men visited Taos and it became local headquarters for some of the fur trading companies. It soon became commonplace to find in the town a variety of people with different backgrounds and nationalities, and most of these foreigners were accepted and welcomed by the Taosenos.

Among those who wandered to Taos were five men who would

Pack train entering Taos, date unknown
Picture courtesy of the Museum of New Mexico, #42868

have much to do with shaping the history of northern New Mexico. They were a product of the fur trade and all were thoroughly acquainted with much of the western frontier. Their names were Bent, St. Vrain, Beaubien, Carson, and Maxwell. Of the group, two of them (St. Vrain and Beaubien) would apply for and receive Mexican citizenship. All of them married Taos women and became well-known and respected leaders of the community.

Charles Bent was born in West Virginia in 1799, one of the eleven children of Silas and Martha Bent. When the boy was six years old the family moved to St. Louis where Silas had been appointed deputy surveyor of the Louisiana Territory. They arrived six days before the Lewis and Clark Expedition returned to that city after exploring to the Pacific. Charles grew up in St. Louis which at the time was situated on the brink of the western frontier and was a crossroads for the many who traveled up and down the Mississippi and Missouri. It was filled with a variety of people on the move to the western lands and the young boy was quickly caught up in the frontier fever. He was sent to Jefferson College in Pennsylvania, then returned to St. Louis after which he joined the Missouri Fur Company. This company was trying to establish itself as a leader in the fur trade on the upper Missouri but was in close competition with the American Fur Company of John Jacob Aster. The Missouri Company lost out and a new trading company was formed, Pilcher & Company, with Bent as one of the partners. This new group struggled against the competition and in an effort to firmly establish a hold on the fur trade decided to send a pack train to a trapper's rendezvous on the Green River in far southwestern Wyoming. The party, which included Charles, his four partners and forty men, traveled up the Missouri, then followed the North Platte to the Sweetwater. There they turned southward, crossed the South Pass and reached their destination in the valley of the Green. Unfortunately for Bent and his company, winter had delayed them, they were forced to cache some of the goods, and other fur traders had already reached the rendezvous. But in a strange twist of fate it so happened that there was another trader at the encampment who had led a group from Taos northward all the way across Colorado and into Wyoming. His name was Ceran St. Vrain. He and Charles quickly became friends and St. Vrain described with enthusiasm the wide open and lucrative Santa Fe market.

Ceran St. Vrain was born near St. Louis in 1802, the descendent of a prominent French family which had come to America and settled in the Louisiana Territory.(4) His father's name was Jacques de Lassus but he had added de St. Vrain to the family surname to clearly distinguish himself from his brother, Charles de Lassus, the lieutenant-governor of the Territory. Jacques owned parcels of land in St. Louis County and established a brewery at Spanish Lake. Not much is known of Ceran's childhood or education. When Jacques died in 1818, the youth of sixteen entered the employment of Bernard Pratte, partner in a fur trading company. Several years were spent in learning the business and Ceran gradually came to be in charge of gathering the men and supplies for the outgoing caravans. Once the Santa Fe Trail opened the young man grew ever more restless to travel west, so in 1824 he arranged financing for his own expedition. The group left in November, was delayed by weather as well as detours to trap beaver and trade with the Indians, and eventually reached New Mexico in March. They crossed the mountains via the Sangre de Christo Pass (La Veta Pass) and came down into Taos from the north.

Ceran immediately took a liking for northern New Mexico and his fondness for Taos would last a lifetime. His basic personality plus the fact that he was both French and Catholic enabled him to rapidly adapt to the culture, customs and people. He quickly became fluent in the native language and made friends easily. Besides, here he did not have to work for a large organization but could be his own man and plan his own future.

Ceran's first years were spent trapping in the mountains, making a quick trip to Missouri and back, and taking part in an expedition that would swing through southern New Mexico, Arizona and southern Colorado. In 1827, in partnership with Sylvestre Pratt, he set out on the long, arduous, and hazardous trading trip to the Green River rendezvous and there he encountered Charles Bent. Strange indeed, that these two who had grown up only a few miles apart in Missouri should come together in a small corner of Wyoming hundreds of miles from home.

When Charles Bent returned to St. Louis from the Green River rendezvous he faced an uncertain future. Pilcher & Co., for which he had labored so hard, was on the verge of bankruptcy and Charles' own finances were in jeopardy. In the course of assaying the future, his mind turned toward the southwest and the markets that lay at the end of the Santa Fe Trail. By vigorous persuasion he was able to raise enough money to purchase goods and then joined a wagon train heading west. On the trip he was accompanied by his younger brother William, and the association between the two would grow ever closer for the remainder of their lives. Although the journey was delayed by an Indian skirmish the group arrived in Santa Fe and within a month had sold their goods for a large profit. The success of this trip fired Bent with enthusiasm for now the future seemed bright, and he never looked back. The following year he again rolled west with several wagons of merchandise, part of a large party of 140 men, 70 wagons, and $120,000 worth of goods. By early August, Bent was in Santa Fe where he quickly disposed of his goods before hurrying back to Missouri. Merchandise was purchased, wagons were assembled, and Charles was again in New Mexico by December--two fast trips in a single season.

While visiting in Taos, Bent was reunited with Ceran St. Vrain and their friendship was fueled by a mutual admiration. Charles also became acquainted with others of the community including Charles Beaubien, a local trader and Kit Carson, who was becoming well known as a mountain man and scout. However it was to

PRELUDE 21

St. Vrain that he turned in planning the future. In 1831 the two decided to form a partnership, thus creating the famous Bent, St. Vrain & Company, which was to become the predominant trading firm in the southern Rockies. The genius of their arrangement was a simple division of labor. Ceran, because of his Taos connections and newly acquired Mexican citizenship, would remain in New Mexico and be in charge of selling and trading the goods. Bent could therefore devote all his time to acquiring merchandise and bringing it by wagon over the Trail. This proved to be both efficient and profitable and the company grew in prestige, power and wealth.

The year following the partnership it was decided to build a large trading post on the Santa Fe Trail as a means toward easier transfer of goods westward. The original idea most likely came from Charles Bent but it was taken up with enthusiasm by both St. Vrain and William Bent, who now was active in the conduct of the company's affairs. A site was chosen on the Arkansas a few miles above the

Bent's fort on the Santa Fe Trail

Charles Bent, fur trader and first governor of the New Mexico Territory
Picture courtesy of the Museum of New Mexico, #7004

Purgatory and plans were laid for a large adobe fort. While Charles was heading west with a huge train of ninety-three wagons, Ceran and William hired over a hundred Mexican workers and led them from Taos to the construction area. The building was completed in 1833 and given the name of Fort William but ever thereafter it was universally known as Bent's Fort.(5) The location was ideal. To the southwest rose the Spanish Peaks which marked the way to the Raton Pass and New Mexico while on the northwest horizon lay Pikes Peak which led to the fur country of Colorado. All this became the domain of Bent, St. Vrain & Co., their trade territory extending from Santa Fe northward as far as the South Platte in northern Colorado. Soon the company would build another post along the South Platte near its juncture with the St. Vrain Creek (north of present day Denver). Completed in 1837, this became known as Fort St. Vrain.

By now, Ceran was well established in Taos, both as a merchant

PRELUDE

and a respected citizen. Though traveling far and wide on behalf of Bent, St. Vrain & Co., his heart was always set on northern New Mexico and Taos had become his home. As the company flourished Charles Bent was able to spend more time in Taos and he seemed to grow increasingly drawn to the community. The true object of this attraction became apparent with the announcement of his betrothal to Ignacia Jaramillo. A member of a prominent Taos family, she was a strikingly beautiful young woman of about twenty. They were married near the end of 1835 and moved into a house just north of the plaza which would remain home to them and their family. Slightly more than a decade hence it would be in this very house that Charles Bent would be killed.(6)

When St. Vrain and Bent had first migrated to Taos they quickly became acquainted with one of the town's leading citizens, a merchant and former mountain man by the name of Charles Beaubien. Beaubien was French-Canadian, having been born in Quebec in 1800 and given the rather imposing name of Charles Hipolyte Trotier Syria de Beaubien. As a young man he began studies preparing

Ceran St. Vrain, partner with Charles Bent in the Bent, St. Vrain and Co.
Picture courtesy of the Museum of New Mexico, #7881

him for the priesthood but then changed his mind and decided his future must lie in another direction. Leaving Canada, he came to the United States and settled in St. Louis. Like many other young men, he succumbed to the lure of the western mountains and joined first the Hudson's Bay Company and later the American Fur Company. As a trapper he wandered over much of the Rockies but eventually turned southward toward New Mexico and found his way to Santa Fe. Here he fell under the spell of the land and its people and decided to remain. Applying for Mexican citizenship, he moved to Taos and opened a store. His trading business was quickly successful and he became a wealthy and respected leader in the community. In 1827 he fell in love with Paulita Lobato, member of an influential Taos family, and they were soon wed. By the time that Bent and St. Vrain came to Taos, Charles Beaubien (now called Carlos by the locals) was a well established figure in the area.

By the middle 1830s the Mexican government was beginning to grow wary of American encroachment. Trade was one thing, obviously beneficial to New Mexicans, but increasing numbers of settlers represented something else, a threat to the Mexican way of life. Each year the number of Americans moving west seemed to grow larger and there appeared no end to the immigration. In addition, Texas was in ferment and a war of independence seemed imminent. This could liberate Texas from Mexican rule and there was already talk of it becoming part of the United States. Some Texans were even beginning to claim that much of the land east of the Rio Grande should belong to Texas. In light of these events the government in Mexico City decided to take steps to protect the territories against American influence. One of the measures undertaken was a revival of the Spanish land grant system. The governor of New Mexico, Manuel Armijo, was instructed to begin making large grants of land to Mexican citizens so that much of the land, and especially the best portions of the land, would remain in native hands. On learning of this program, Charles Beaubien decided to apply for one of these land grants. Although he was indeed a Mexican citizen, in some ways he was yet an outsider and foreigner so he felt it necessary to strengthen his position. He joined forces with a well known citizen of Santa Fe, Guadalupe Miranda, who was not only highly respected but also a man who carried considerable weight with governor Armijo. Miranda had come north from Chihuahua and opened a Catholic school in Santa Fe. Later he had served as headmaster of the Santa Fe schools and for a time was secretary to the governor. Beaubien and Miranda applied for a grant consisting of a large area on the eastern slopes of the Sangre de Christo mountains to include much of the upper watershed of the Canadian River. Obviously, much insider groundwork had been laid, for the grant was approved within only three days and thus there came into being the vast Beaubien-Miranda Land Grant, the largest of all the Mexican land grants. At the time there was no survey, all boundaries being based on natural landmarks and vague descriptions. In the late 19th century when an official survey was carried out by government surveyors, the grant was found to consist of over 1.7 million acres, an area more than twice the size of Rhode Island. Thirty years after the grant was acquired it would come to play a vital role in the history of the Red River Valley.

Beaubien, encouraged by the apparent ease of obtaining this grant, decided to apply for additional land. Since he himself was ineligible for a second grant, he arranged a partnership between his son Narciso (a minor and only 13) and Stephen Lee, a well known citizen of Taos and Beaubien's brother-in-law (Lee's wife was the sister of Paulita Beaubien). The grant was awarded by Armijo, creating the Sangre de Christo Land Grant, comprising about one million acres and being the second largest of the Mexican land grants. It would later play a part in the gold rush days of Red River.(7)

The most famous of all the mountain men who settled in Taos was Christopher (Kit) Carson. A combination of trapper, trader, explorer, scout, hunter, Indian agent, and soldier, he was the quintessential American frontiersman. During his thirties he served as scout for the government expeditions of John C. Fremont and this brought his name to the attention of the public. Later, a series of articles about him appeared in *Harper's New Monthly Magazine* and as a result he became a national hero.

Carson was born in Madison County, Kentucky in 1809 but his family moved to Missouri when the boy was only a year of age. The large and growing family (eventually Lindsey and Rebecca Carson would have eight children) settled on a farm in the Boonslick area. Here they were somewhat isolated and subject to all the difficulties of frontier life including occasional Indian raids. Kit received very little formal education and throughout his life was unable to read or write. Nevertheless he possessed a great deal of native intelligence and was a quick learner.

When Carson was nine years old his father Lindsey was killed in an accident and four years later Rebecca remarried. The older brothers began to drift away and at age fifteen Kit became apprenticed to a saddler in Franklin. This work was tedious and confining to the boy who had spent much of his life in the outdoors. Besides, he was beginning to develop the wanderlust, a common affliction of the young men of his day. Part of this was fueled by the tales told by his two older brothers who had already ventured westward. Some of it came from the many trappers, traders, and mountain men who frequented Franklin, which at the time was the jumping off place for those heading to the western lands.

In 1826, at the age of sixteen, Kit ran away from home and joined a wagon train headed for Santa Fe. By this time he was a skillful hunter and excellent horseman, so was able to be useful to the group. By chance, the caravan captain was Ceran St. Vrain. To a young man of this impressionable age it was a great adventure and an exciting trip. The caravan reached Santa Fe without mishap and Carson traveled on to Taos, which at the time had a population of

PRELUDE 27

3,600 people. He quickly adapted to the community and its people, learning the native language and the local customs. Though Kit would spend much of his life in wandering and traveling the western United States, it was to Taos that he always returned, the place he would call home, and the site where he would eventually be buried.

Over the next decade Carson would embark on a series of trapping excursions, trading trips, and explorations that would cover amazing distances and would last many months at a time. The Ewing Expedition of 1829 left Taos and traveled through what is now Colorado, Utah, Arizona, and California, eventually reaching Los Angeles and San Francisco. Extensive trips were later made into the upper reaches of the Missouri, exploring the Yellowstone and Powder Rivers. One long journey led across Idaho to Oregon and Washington, then turned south to California before returning to New Mexico. During this time Carson honed his skills as a trapper, hunter

Kit Carson home in Taos, now the Kit Carson Museum
Picture courtesy of the Museum of New Mexico, photographer H. Parkhurst, #7133

and explorer. He met a variety of Indian tribes (Sioux, Shoshone, Flatheads, Nez Perces, Crow) and learned enough of their dialects to be able to communicate. During these years his reputation as a scout grew ever greater. In 1842 he was selected by John Charles Fremont to guide a government expedition through the West to California. It so happened that another young man from Taos was hired to be a hunter for the group. His name was Lucien Maxwell and he and Carson would become lifelong friends.

Maxwell was originally from Illinois and member of a rather prominent family, his grandfather, Pierre Menard having been lieu-

Lucien Maxwell, owner of the vast Maxwell Land Grant
Picture courtesy of the Museum of New Mexico, #50592

PRELUDE

tenant governor of the state. Lucien, like others of his age, headed west as a young man and hired on with the American Fur Company. The next two years were spent in the Rocky Mountains becoming proficient as a trapper, trader, and mountain man. In 1839 he entered the employment of Bent, St. Vrain & Co. and spent time in Colorado before eventually wandering to Taos. Here he fell in love with Luz Beaubien, the eldest daughter of Charles and Paulita Beaubien. Lucien and Luz were wed in 1842, the same year that Maxwell and Carson served with Fremont, and following that expedition, Lucien went to work for his father-in-law in the Taos trading establishment. Carson also returned to Taos and in the following year married Josefa Jaramillo, the sister of Charles Bent's wife, Ignacia.(8) Romance must have been in the air, for shortly thereafter Ceran St. Vrain also found a wife, a younger daughter of Charles Beaubien.(9) Thus, Maxwell and St. Vrain became brothers-in-law as did Bent and Carson.

During the 1840s, relations between the United States and Mexico became increasingly strained. The Americans looked longingly upon the Southwest and California for their own, and the policy of Manifest Destiny was in full swing. The independence of Texas and its subsequently becoming a part of the United States only fueled the flames of conflict so that war seemed not only likely but imminent. Rumors of war were heard in Washington and St. Louis but also were rampant in Santa Fe and Mexico City. In May of 1846 an official declaration of war was issued by Congress and the conflict began.

Gen. Stephen Watts Kearny was given command of the Army of the West (a rather grandiose title for a force consisting of only 1700 men) and ordered to invade the New Mexico Territory, which at the time consisted of the entire Southwest. He assembled a force and supply trains at St. Louis and began the imposing trek of eight hundred miles to Santa Fe. Although the march was slow and haphazard, its problems paled in comparison to the chaos in Santa Fe.

Gov. Armijo, receiving very little aid from Mexico City and unable to gain support from his Indian allies, tried in various ways to mount a military defense. Nothing seemed to work and his plans for a confrontation with the Americans began to unravel. As Kearny grew ever closer he became more desperate. Finally, Armijo and many of the Mexican citizens (including Guadalupe Miranda) fled south to Mexico enabling the Americans to make a bloodless entry into Santa Fe. New Mexico was now a part of the United States. Kearny's first act was to appoint a provisional government consisting of Charles Bent as governor and Donaciano Vigil as lieutenant governor. Charles Beaubien became a judge of the superior court; in Taos Stephen Lee was recognized as sheriff and Cornelio Vigil remained as Prefect.

Unfortunately, Kearny's easy conquest of Santa Fe led him to misread the mood of many of the Mexicans and Indians, especially those in Taos. He assumed that New Mexico had been completely pacified and therefore he might turn his eyes toward California, the conquest of which would bring fame and honor. Within slightly more than a month of arriving in Santa Fe, Kearny set out for California taking with him Kit Carson as a guide. Colonel Sterling Price, commanding a small force, was left in charge in Santa Fe. Soon there was increasing unrest among some of the Mexicans and Indians and a plot against the Americans was hatched. Simultaneous uprisings were planned for both Santa Fe and Taos with the Pueblo Indians playing a major role. As rumors of general turmoil continued to grow, Charles Bent, now governor, decided to travel to Taos in an effort to calm the waters and reassure the Taos Pueblo Indians. In January he set out, refusing a military escort which he thought might only add to the growing tension. Included in his party were two youngsters, Pablo Jaramillo (brother to Ignacia Bent and Josefa Carson) and Narciso Beaubien, the son of Charles Beaubien. On reaching Taos, the group discovered gangs of hostile Indians and Mexicans in the streets but were able to proceed to their homes.

As night wore on many of the Taos Indians drifted into town and a large mob began to form. It finally attacked the jail and Stephen Lee, the sheriff, fled to a nearby housetop where he was caught and butchered. Prefect Cornelio Vigil attempted to reason with the mob but it turned on him, piercing him with arrows and knives. Circuit Attorney James Leal was shot full of arrows, blinded, then scalped while yet alive; he wandered the streets until he died. The mob then moved to Governor Bent's house and attempted to break in through the door and roof. Charles attempted to reason with the attackers by shouting through the door. Meanwhile, the women (including Ignacia, Josefa Carson, and the Bent's daughter, Teresina) set about digging through the wall of a back room and into an adjoining house. As the women were making their escape through the hole, the door was broken down and Bent was shot with arrows. He attempted to crawl to the adjoining room but his head was dashed against the floor and then he was scalped. The women were caught and though left unharmed, were forced to remain in the house with the body of Charles Bent for over twenty-four hours.(10)

Meanwhile the mob continued its rampage through the town and many of the stores of American traders were ransacked and burned. The two boys, Pablo Jaramillo and Narciso Beaubien, were found attempting to hide under a pile of hay and were promptly killed. At Arroyo Hondo the Turley distillery was attacked and after a period of fighting, Turley was killed along with several of his men.(11)

When the killing began, several horsemen slipped out of the town and galloped to Santa Fe, carrying news of the open rebellion. Lieutenant Price promptly started his troops on the road northward to Taos and accompanying them was a force of sixty-five volunteer mountain men raised by Ceran St. Vrain. Meanwhile a large group of Mexicans and Taos Pueblo Indians had started down the Rio Grande to attack Santa Fe. The two forces met at Embudo where the rebels were soundly defeated. The Mexicans fled in all directions while the Indians retreated toward Taos and eventually concentrated in the Taos Pueblo. Price's pursuit was both rapid and relentless as he pushed his troops through the town and the additional three miles to the Pueblo. Here the siege began. After two days of fierce fighting the walls were breached and Americans poured into the buildings. Many of the defenders were killed and those trying to flee were cut down by St. Vrain's men who were mounted on horseback. As the smoke finally cleared the Pueblo counted its losses at about 150 dead.

When the fighting subsided, leaders of the rebellion were rounded up and brought to trial. The outcome was not much in doubt since one of the judges was Charles Beaubien and among the jurors were: Elliott Lee, relative of the slain sheriff; Lucien Maxwell, brother-in-law of Narciso; and George Bent, a brother to Charles. As a result, fifteen of the rebel conspirators were convicted and promptly hung.(12)

Following this episode there was very little fighting in New Mexico. While Gen. Taylor assembled an army in Texas and invaded northern Mexico, American troops under Winfield Scott went ashore at Vera Cruz and besieged Mexico City. The fall of this city brought an end to the war. The treaty of peace resulted in Mexico ceding to the United States all of its territories extending from Texas to the Pacific. This vast region would later include the states of New Mexico, Arizona, Nevada, California, Utah, and a portion of Colorado. After the war New Mexico became a Territory of the U.S. with an appointed governor, but for a period of time much of the administration and control of the area was carried out by the Army. A number of forts were subsequently built and this included Fort Union in eastern New Mexico which was located so as to provide protection for travelers on the Santa Fe Trail.

The Treaty of Guadalupe Hidalgo stipulated that land titles previously held by Mexican citizens would be recognized under American law. Therefore Charles Beaubien continued to retain one-half ownership of the Beaubien-Miranda Land Grant and since Miranda had fled to Mexico, Charles was in effect the sole proprietor of the property. One of the requirements of the land grants was that the new owners must attempt to colonize and develop the land. Beaubien decided to proceed with this and turned to his son-in-law, Lucien Maxwell, to fulfill the task. As regards the Sangre de Christo Grant, after the death of Narciso Beaubien the boy's half interest reverted to his father. Since Stephen Lee had also been killed, Charles Beaubien purchased the other interest from Lee's heirs and became sole owner. Whether it was the death of his son or the result of other factors, Beaubien lost interest in this land grant and later it was sold to William Gilpin, the first territorial governor of Colorado.

Lucian Maxwell and his wife, Luz, decided to move to the Beaubien-Miranda Land Grant and make it their home. In the company of several Mexican settler families and with a pack train of mules, Maxwell set out from Taos. The group followed the old trail eastward that led up Taos Creek to Palo Flachedo Pass (present-day US 64) and entered into the southern end of the Moreno Valley. Instead of turning north toward the Cimarron Canyon, they proceeded due east over the mountains and came down into the Rayado Canyon. It was on the Rayado that Lucien began building a home and ranch. A rather large house was constructed along with barns, corrals, and other buildings and a herd of cattle was brought in from Bent's Fort. In 1849 Kit Carson joined Maxwell on the Rayado, building a house of his own and planning to make this a home for Josefa and their children. For a while there was the threat of Indian raids but the following year the Army established a post at Rayado which was assigned two companies of dragoons. The presence of these soldiers brought security to the area and, though they would later be moved thirty miles south to Ft. Union, there were no subsequent problems.

Over the next few years Maxwell was able to convince other

The Maxwell House was located in what is now the town of Cimarron. It burned in 1922.
Picture courtesy of the Museum of New Mexico, photographer E. Troutman, #147388

settlers to come to the area and he brought in additional animals. His ranching activities began to generate considerable income and this was augmented by the selling and renting of land. He opened a trading store to supply travelers along the Santa Fe Trail and it proved to be a very successful venture. When he was able to obtain a contract to supply meat and grain to the Army, his wealth was assured and continued to grow. After the death of Charles Beaubien, Maxwell bought out the surviving heirs of Miranda as well as the other Beaubien children so that he and Luz became sole owners of the grant. Henceforth, the property was called the Maxwell Land Grant and constituted the largest individually owned piece of real estate in the history of the United States.(13)

After several years on the Rayado, in 1857 Maxwell decided to move his headquarters northward and chose a site on the Cimarron

The Aztec Mill built by Lucien Maxwell. It is located in present day Cimarron and serves as a museum.
Picture courtesy of the J. R. Pierce collection

River only a few miles off the Santa Fe Trail (the present site of the town of Cimarron). Here he built a large mansion suitable for a man of his wealth and added various buildings, barns, corrals, and a large gristmill. His horse and cattle herds grew to very large size and it is said that at one time he grazed a hundred thousand head of sheep. He continued to prosper from the contracts to supply meat, grain, and flour to the Army, and also traded goods to those passing by on the Trail. Maxwell's ranch became a welcome rest stop for travelers and he frequently offered meals and lodging to visitors so that it became commonplace for there to be twenty or more guests at his evening table. It was at the Cimarron ranch that the Maxwells raised their large family consisting of five daughters (Odile, Virginia, Sophia, Emilia, and Paula) and one son (Peter Menard). All of the children married and produced twenty-one grandchildren.(14)

In spite of all the activity in and around Taos during the first half of the 19th century, there was little or no penetration of the Red River Valley by either Mexicans or Americans prior to 1860. Certainly there were no settlements and if any wanderers ventured here we have no record of it. One would suspect that trappers might have explored the area in search of beaver, but if so, they left no mark. However, Native American Indians had roamed the mountains of northern New Mexico for nearly three hundred years and undoubtedly had visited the Valley and surrounding mountains. There were three different groups of Indians that were quite likely indigenous to this particular area--Utes, Jicarilla Apaches, and Taos Pueblo Indians.

The Utes, related by language to the Shoshone people, migrated from Utah south and eastward into Colorado where they wandered the mountains, valleys, and plateaus of the southern Rockies. At the time of their reaching northern New Mexico (probably around 1700), they were a warlike people and frequently carried on raiding parties against the Jicarilla Apaches. Their society was based on hunting of game and the gathering of berries, fruits, and plants. In New Mexico, for reasons not completely clear, they became much more peaceful and actually befriended the Jicarillas. After a time, intermarriage between the two tribes became common and they often cooperated with one another against common enemies. It was not unusual for Utes to serve alongside Spanish soldiers as scouts or auxiliaries.

The introduction of the Spanish horse into Ute culture greatly increased their mobility and range of territory, thus enabling them to retain a way of life based on hunting. They remained a wandering people, spending summers in the high meadows and wintering in the lowlands along the base of the mountains. Although the Utes were considered peaceful, raiding remained a common practice whereby they could obtain horses or other animals for trading or to supplement their food supply. In fact, as late as 1845 a raiding party

PRELUDE 37

of Utes drove off several hundred sheep and cattle from a ranch near Taos.

Although there are no definite records of Ute Indians in the Red River Valley, their presence in the surrounding areas is well-known. Ute Park along the Cimarron River was a favorite summer camping ground. Both Utes and Jicarilla Apaches were involved in several raids at the vicinity of Maxwell's ranch on the Rayado and later a band of Utes attacked Maxwell and a group of fourteen men at the Raton Pass (in the fight Lucien received a severe neck wound). Utes traded in Taos and Santa Fe and were often seen at the Taos Pueblo. And it would be a Ute Indian who would play an important role in the discovery of gold in the Moreno Valley.

The Jicarilla Apaches were descendants of an Athabascan language group of Indians originally found in central Canada. Around the year 1200 they began a migration southward and slowly moved down the Great Plains through Nebraska, Kansas, Colorado, and finally New Mexico. They encountered the horse, gradually adapted to a culture based on hunting of buffalo and thus, in some ways resembled the other Plains Indians. About the year 1700 these Apaches came under increased pressure from the much more warlike Comanches and were forced westward into the Sangre de Christo mountains. Here they came to be influenced by the Pueblo Indians and learned to raise crops so that their culture became a combination of hunting and agriculture. Generally they lived along the foothills and in the low valleys where a variety of crops were produced such as corn, beans, peas, pumpkins, and tobacco. Hunting for food required extensive searching of the mountains for game and they explored and wandered over most of the Sangre de Christos.

The Jicarillas were generally looked upon as peaceful, and often could be found at Taos and Santa Fe where they came to trade goods. Nevertheless, many of the young men continued to carry out raids in order to obtain horses, cattle and sheep. Some of these activities were directed against the wagon trains along the Santa Fe Trail, but raids on ranches and local settlements were common. In this way the Indians were able to supplement their basic subsistence.

In 1861 an Indian Agency was established at Maxwell's ranch on the Cimarron to serve the Utes and Jicarilla Apaches. It was the intention of the U.S. Government to provide them with meat, grain, and other items such as blankets, but often this goal fell short because of insufficient appropriations. More than once, Maxwell made up the deficits by providing goods from his own stores and as a result, the ranch at Cimarron was free from raids by these Indians.

The Taos Pueblo Indians had been in place for hundreds of years and the legal ownership of their land had been assured through land grants awarded by the king of Spain. In contrast to the Utes and Apaches who were wanderers, the Taos Indians lived in a permanent community which had grown into the large and rather complex Taos Pueblo. Here their society was based upon agriculture and the raising of a variety of crops some of which could be traded. The men also engaged in hunting and must have roamed over much of the adjacent mountains including the Red River valley. It is also important to note that Blue Lake, the ceremonial site for the Taos Indians, is located over the mountain ridge and only a mile or two from the East Fork of the Red River. Thus, the entire Red River area was undoubtedly familiar ground to these people.

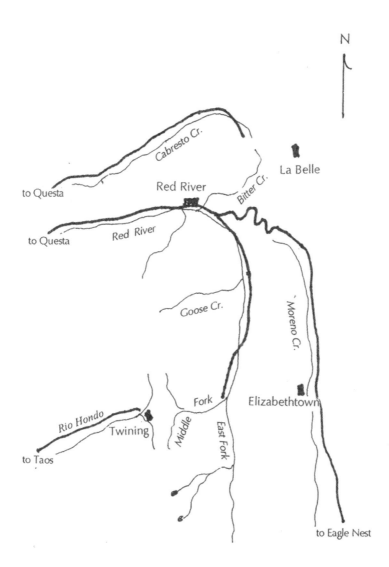

Map showing the early gold camps of Twining, Elizabethtown, La Belle, and Red River

40

GOLD FEVER
(1860 - 1910)

About the time of the American Civil War, gold was discovered in northern New Mexico and for the next five decades this would drive the economy, settlement, and culture of the entire region. Prospectors and miners from far and wide poured into the country and like the mountain men before them, they were mostly young, single, and in search of riches. They would roam the mountains searching in all the canyons and valleys as well as along various streams and rivers in search of the big strike. Almost all the land was explored out so that even today, those who wander the back country are often amazed to find old mines and diggings in many obscure and out of the way places. The major activity came to be located in four areas: Amizette and Twining on the upper Rio Hondo; Elizabethtown in the Moreno Valley; La Belle on Comanche Creek; and the Red River Valley.

On the map draw a circle with its center on the town of Red River, and having a radius of fifteen miles. All four of the mining towns would lie within this circle, indicating their close proximity to one another. This is somewhat misleading since the straight line distances might be only a few miles but there were intervening mountains and canyons which made travel difficult. Thus the distance between Red River and Twining might be only twelve miles but this involved climbing over a mountain range of eleven to twelve thousand feet. Although such a trip could be carried out on foot or horseback, it would be totally impossible in winter. In contrast, the same journey by wagon road through Questa and Arroyo Hondo meant a forty or fifty mile trip. Similarly, the direct distance from Twining to Elizabethtown was less than fifteen miles, but wagons going by road were forced to travel through Taos, climb up Taos Creek valley to Palo Flechedo Pass, descend to the lower Moreno

Valley and thence north to Elizabethtown, a distance close to fifty miles.(1)

In the early days before there were many roads, travel between the mining camps was carried out on foot or by horseback (and only in summer). In fact, it was commonplace for miners or prospectors to move back and forth between the mining districts depending on which one seemed to have the most promising gold strikes at a given time. As roads were opened, travel became much easier and eventually stage service was established between all the towns.

The four mining districts developed at different times between 1860 and 1895. Because of its proximity to Taos, the Rio Hondo was explored early, sometime after 1850. The Moreno Valley strike took place in 1866 and Elizabethtown was established the following year. It was not until 1894 that La Belle was founded and the town of Red River came into existence shortly thereafter. By the late 1890s all of the districts were active and the various towns seemed prosperous and growing. Soon thereafter they began to wane and by 1910 only Red River and Elizabethtown remained, and the latter would soon disappear.

All of the mining areas faced similar, and at times almost unsolvable, difficulties. With a few noted exceptions, the ore was usually very inconsistent in assay. An apparent rich vein would be uncovered, resulting in jubilation and optimism, but further digging would reveal only low-grade ore which produced tiny amounts of gold. As a result, in many places it became necessary to dig many tons of rock in order to reap any significant income. Another problem was the scarcity of investment capital, which was necessary to develop the mines. It is one thing to discover gold, but removing it from the ground and then shipping it to a smelter is something on an entirely different scale. The development and operation of a mine of any size called for a significant outlay of money. Large machinery had to be ordered and then shipped in by wagon over very crude and

GOLD FEVER

mountainous roads. A crew of miners had to be employed in the mine to dig and remove the ore. Finally, the transportation cost of shipping the ore to a smelter had to be paid. The cost of all these operations represented up front money which could only be recouped when the ore was finally smelted. As a result of these large costs, the ordinary miners and prospectors wound up selling their claims to speculators who would purchase a number of claims and then attempt to attract outside investors from as far away as Denver, Chicago, or St. Louis.

The most difficult problem, which eventually proved to be insurmountable, was that of transporting the ore to the nearest smelter, located at Denver (later at Colorado Springs). Wagons were used and the existing roads over the mountains were rough, unimproved, and frequently impassable in winter. The nearest railroads were located at Springer, Catskill (west of Raton), Tres Piedras, and Antonito, many miles from the gold fields. Various schemes were put forward in an effort to lure the railroads closer to the mining districts, but with a single exception, these proved fruitless.(2) To a large extent, it was the high transportation costs which doomed much of the mining efforts in northern New Mexico.

Amizette and Twining on the Rio Hondo
(1860 - 1905)

In the years preceding the Civil War prospecting was carried out along the Rio Hondo, located a few miles north of Taos, and enough gold dust was washed from the stream that a number of claims came to be staked in the area. By 1865 there were over a hundred claims registered, most of them within two or three miles of Arroyo Hondo. Among the prospects were claims by Ceran St. Vrain and also by Kit Carson, organized under the name of the Kit Carson

Lode. In spite of extensive searching, the ore was low-grade and very uneven in distribution, so that many of the miners became discouraged. When news came that rich strikes had been made in the Moreno Valley, a few miles to the east, prospectors began to drift to that area. Soon only a few miners remained along the Rio Hondo and these men gradually began to move up the river into the mountains. In 1868 there was renewed activity when gold was found near California Gulch. The Arroyo Hondo Mining and Ditch Company was organized and money was raised from a group of Taos investors. A stamp mill was erected and a team of fifteen men was put to work recovering ore. However, after working for nine months, only enough gold was produced to barely cover the initial investment and the company was forced to stop operations.

During the early 1870s prospecting continued, but only on a small scale. During that decade, however, there began the Colorado gold rush which created a renewed interest in mining activities throughout New Mexico and the other western regions. As a result, a wave of new individuals appeared along the Rio Hondo and these included Colonel William Craig, William Fraser, and the two Anderson brothers, William and Alexander. Craig had been stationed in Taos during his tour with the regular army and following his discharge had returned to the area and quickly staked twenty claims near the head of the Rio Hondo. The Andersons began mining activities on the lower portion of the river but eventually moved up the canyon and recovered gold not far from Col. Craig. Fraser, who had learned of the gold prospects through a chance meeting with the Andersons, came to the area and would prove to be the most well-known of all those in the Rio Hondo region.

In the early 1880s further strikes brought renewed interest in the area, creating an influx of new miners as well as fresh capital. This was heightened by the National Mining Exposition at Denver in 1882, at which the Taos mining district presented an exhibit. Col. Craig opened the Highland Chief and silver ore was discovered at his Pottsville mine. The Ophir mine, located near the north fork of the Rio Hondo, was expected to become profitable as was the Bull of the Woods. Fraser staked multiple claims at the head of the river and began looking for investors, hoping to sell part ownership. His search was rewarded with the sale of sixteen claims to a pair of Ohio men for twenty thousand dollars. Other investors showed interest including two from Elizabethtown, James Lowrey and James Lynch, who acquired part interest in the Ophir and Bull of the Woods. Craig was able to raise enough money to put on a crew of thirty miners at the Highland Chief. Prospectors began to explore the surrounding area and a few crossed over the divide into the West Fork of the Red River where several claims were staked.(3)

In spite of all the activity, there was not much real development or production. The ore was very uneven in grade and transportation costs for shipping out of the mountains all but eliminated any serious profits. Gradually, pessimism set in, investment capital began to dry up and many of the miners began to leave. Fraser remained enthusiastic, convinced that the area indeed contained riches, and coupled with this was his uncanny ability to find and interest investors. He continued the search for additional claims and even built a toll road from Arroyo Hondo to the headwaters of the river (the charge was twenty-five cents a wagon).

During the fall of 1893, Fraser's perseverance paid off when he and Al Helphenstine discovered very rich gold and silver ore on the upper Rio Hondo, setting off a new boom in the area. Miners flocked to the canyon once again, and cabins began to appear. A townsite was organized, located in the mountains not far below the junction of the two forks of the river. Here, Helphenstine began construction of a hotel and other merchants soon followed. The town was given the name of Amizette in honor of Helphenstine's wife, the first woman in the camp. Within a matter of months the town contained more than 150 people, a general merchandise store built by the Gusdorf brothers, a restaurant, meat market, blacksmith shop,

The hotel at Amizette built by Al Helphenstine, picture taken about 1895
Picture courtesy of the Museum of New Mexico, #132446

and of course, a saloon. W.W. Follett, a civil and mining engineer, arrived in the camp and soon was followed by J.E. Lacome, recently appointed as deputy sheriff. The toll road from Arroyo Hondo was improved and stage service was established between Amizette and Tres Piedras. It was not long before a number of rumors began to circulate that rail service to the Rio Hondo was being planned.(4)

Several companies were organized and these included the Taos Mountain Mining and Milling Company backed by a group of Chicago investors, the Rio Hondo Placer Mining Company organized by a Denver group, and the Lucas Gold Placer Mining Company owned by a wealthy St. Louis firm. The Chicago company purchased several claims from William Fraser and soon uncovered fine ore containing gold, silver, and copper. Prospectors began to explore Long Canyon on the north fork of the river and soon were working the west side of Gold Hill where several mines were opened.

For the next two years the upper Rio Hondo was alive with activity and Amizette saw a steady stream of prospectors and visitors. But nowhere was the big strike, the mother lode that would produce untold riches. The ore continued to be spotty, transportation remained a problem and the various companies began to run out of capital. As a result miners began to leave for other areas, particularly La Belle, where there were glowing reports of new gold discoveries. The number of people in the valley began to slowly decline but a few of the faithful remained and continued to work their claims. Among these, of course, was William Fraser who persistently searched for new prospects. He concentrated on that part of the canyon where the Lake Fork joined the main river and worked the west side of the mountain that came to be called Fraser Hill and later Fraser Mountain.(5) After sinking several tunnels he realized that the gold which was present was mixed with copper. In fact, there was so much copper that it seemed likely that healthy profits could be made by concentrating on this metal alone. In order to produce copper his first requirement was a reduction mill and this meant finding investment capital. For Fraser, this never seemed to be much of an obstacle.

Two companies were organized, the Rio Hondo Copper Mining Company and the Cristobal Gold and Silver Mining Company, backed by three Taos men, one of whom had connections with an English investment group. Fraser was to be provided with $100,000 to purchase a smelter and build the housing for it. Men were hired, timber was cut to provide lumber, and building was begun. All of this new activity brought miners back to the area and created interest in other properties. The Gusdorf brothers reopened their Shoshone mine on Gold Hill and were followed by others who began searching in Long Canyon and on Gold Hill. Several mines were opened amid a new wave of enthusiasm and these included the Iron Dyke. By the time the shaft of the Iron Dyke had reached 350 feet it was estimated to contain a million dollars of low-grade ore. The difficulty faced by the owners was to find a process which could extract the gold cheaply enough to yield these riches. It was hoped that a new electrical process could be perfected that would accomplish this, but in the end, the new method did not work. The owners became discouraged and closed the mine.

In the meantime, Fraser had received $60,000 of his expected money and had almost completed the buildings to house his mill. In a sudden reversal of fortune he learned that the investors were not able to raise any additional money for further operations. Therefore the smelter was not ordered and the operation was gradually shut down.

As mining activity continued at a slow pace around Amizette and in Long Canyon, Fraser, not one to be discouraged, set out to find new investors. This turned out to be a difficult undertaking and it was not until two years later that he appeared to be back in business. In 1899, the Rio Hondo Copper Company was announced, backed by wealthy men from New York and Montana. Fraser was paid over a hundred thousand dollars for thirteen claims, and he immediately went to work improving and extending the mines. By the following summer, thirty men were at work on the property, digging shafts, erecting buildings and improving the road to Arroyo Hondo. The Company had now spent an additional eighty thosand dollars and in order to raise further capital decided to reoganize. A group of New Jersey investors headed by Albert Twing purchased a controlling interest and in 1901 incorporated as the Fraser Mountain Copper Company. Within a short time there was a flurry of activity. A smelter was ordered, the work force was increased to sixty men, and several buildings were built, including the large four-story mill which would house the smelter.

By this time almost all activity in the valley was centered at the Fraser Mountain property and Amizette had become almost vacant. A new townsite was established at the junction of the Lake Fork and the North Fork (the site of today's Taos Ski Area) and was given the name of Twining. It soon became a beehive of activity and attracted a number of newcomers. Water was piped from high in the mountains and used to power the cable tramway, which would bring ore from the mines down to the valley floor. The water also powered an electric generator which ran a compressor for the air drills which had been installed. Cabins and bunkhouses were built, telephone lines were laid, the Twining Hotel went up, and the number of people in the town rose to about two hundred. By the summer of 1903, the smelting machinery--rollers, crush- ers, furnaces--had been installed and the feverish activity had reached its climax.

The first "run" began and although it had to be stopped because of a broken pulley, a significant amount of copper was produced. On the second trial the ore froze, solidifying within the machinery. This calamity, which had brought ruin to other mining camps, probably was related to the basic chemical makeup of the ore which led to a heavy precipitation within the molten rock. All work was suspended while miners began the laborious task of chipping out the solid ore and rock with picks. When all of the debris had been removed another trial run was begun. To everyone's great disappointment, the ore promptly froze again, spelling defeat to the miners, operators, and investors. Within a few months the town had largely emptied, the Fraser Mountain Copper Company was in receivership and Twining had declared bankruptcy.

The mining district held on for another year or two largely through the efforts of the American Consolidated Mines Company which continued working claims in the Lake Fork Canyon. After spending three hundred thousand dollars without a major return, this company suspended its operation. Fraser tried to recover by again raising capital but was unsuccessful. In desperation he formed a partnership with Jack Bidwell and Clarence Probert of Taos, but almost from the beginning he was dissatisfied with his partners and hard feelings developed. Fraser brought suit against them but lost in court. Several years later, the still embittered Fraser encountered Bidwell, pulled a gun and opened fire. In the ensuing gun fight Fraser was killed.

For nearly fifty years the valley remained dormant and virtually deserted. The old buildings gradually collapsed or were demolished. The great mill, upon which so much labor and hope had been expended, began to decay and then was destroyed by fire. It was not until the 1950s that Ernie Blake came to the valley and selected the area of Twining as the site for his winter playground, the Taos Ski Area. Since then, each winter thousands of visitors come to enjoy the fast runs, scenic beauty, and fresh mountain air, while deep beneath the snow the old mines lie asleep and unattended.

The Moreno Valley and Elizabethtown
(1866 - 1920)

In the late summer of 1866, the year following Lee's surrender at Appomattox, a Ute Indian traveled to Fort Union in order to trade furs. With him he carried some greenish rocks which he thought might be of some value. After exchanging furs, he showed the rocks to Col. William Moore, the fort's sutler, who immediately recognized that they were copper ore. Inquiry revealed that the rocks had been collected on the slopes of Baldy Mountain in the Moreno Valley. With visions of wealth from a great copper mine, Moore formed The Copper Company in partnership with William Kroenig and John Buck. Three prospectors--Larry Bronson, Peter Kisinger, and R.P. Kelly--were selected to explore the area. The trio left Ft. Union, journeyed to Maxwell's Ranch, and then followed the Cimarron Canyon up to the Moreno Valley, a long open valley running north and south, dominated on its eastern side by Baldy Mountain. The men turned and followed Willow Creek which drains the south slope of Baldy. While his two companions were setting up camp and cooking supper, Kelly, for want of something to do, began to pan the stream. Much to his surprise, gold was present in large amounts. The three men promptly forgot about copper and began to search the surrounding streams, gulches, and gravel beds. Almost everywhere they looked, there was gold.

The approach of winter, heralded by a severe snow storm, forced the three prospectors to leave the valley. They retreated back down the Cimarron and returned to Ft. Union, planning to return in the spring. Although the men had agreed to keep their discovery a secret, over winter the word leaked out of this apparent major gold strike. The news spread quickly in all directions and the following year hundreds of miners and prospectors from the adjoining states and territories flocked to the area. They rapidly staked claims over much of Baldy, along Willow Creek, and in Grouse Gulch, Michigan Gulch, and Humbug Gulch.

By summer there were several hundred people in the area and it was decided to establish a townsite, located on the western side of the valley. The town was named for Elizabeth, the four year old daughter of John Moore who was a principal organizer of the community. Thus, Elizabethtown (or E-town as it came to be called), became the first incorporated town in New Mexico and later was chosen as the county seat of the newly formed Colfax county. It

Elizabethtown in 1897
Picture courtesy of the Museum of New Mexico, photo by Aultman, #148101

continued to grow rapidly and within another year was estimated to contain somewhere between 2,000 and 7,000 people. The claim was made that it had become the third largest town in New Mexico, behind only Santa Fe and Taos.(6)

At the time, the entire area was a part of the Maxwell Land Grant, owned by Lucien Maxwell who sold and rented parcels of land in and around Elizabethtown in addition to requiring a fee from the prospectors for filing their claims. At one time he attempted to establish a town at the point where the North Moreno and the Cieneguilla creeks came together to form the Cimarron River. This was given the grand title of Virginia City, named for one of the Maxwell daughters. Though lots were sold and a few cabins begun, the scheme failed and the town was soon empty and never recovered. Lucien invested in several other enterprises in the Valley as well as a few mining ventures. On the eastern slopes of Baldy evidence of rich ore had been uncovered by Matthew Lynch and two other prospectors. As a result, Maxwell opened several mines including the Aztec, Montezuma, and French Henry. The Aztec proved to be a very rich mine and in a little over six months produced more than one hundred thousand dollars in gold. Maxwell would soon become the richest man in the Territory.

Around E-town the gold was found mixed in the sand and gravel, so in this area placer mining was employed, a process consisting of washing the sand with water. Within a short time another method came into use, hydraulic mining, which had been developed in the California gold fields. Its use in the Moreno Valley was introduced and pioneered by Matthew Lynch who had extensive holdings in Grouse Gulch and along Willow Creek. Hydraulic mining consisted of using high pressure water hoses connected to a large nozzle which directed a strong flow of water into the sides of the gulch. The mixture of sand and water was then collected by a series of long sluice boxes from which the gold could be collected.

Both the placer and hydraulic methods required a large amount

GOLD FEVER 53

Hydraulic mining at the Lynch Placer. The man in the top hat is said to be Matthew Lynch.
Picture courtesy of the Museum of New Mexico, #14860

of water which initially was drawn from the North Moreno Creek. With the increasing numbers of miners the volume of water in the creek proved insufficient especially as midsummer approached and the snow melt waned. By August many of the claims could no longer be worked and a search began for additional supplies of water. Maxwell hired Captain N.S. Davis, a retired Army Engineer living at Ft. Union, to survey the entire region for a solution. Davis, without benefit of maps, roads, or trails, traveled westward across the ridge and into the Red River watershed and explored that river and all its tributaries. He developed a plan to build a large ditch which would divert water from the Red River across the mountains and into the Moreno Valley. As a result, a company was organized to proceed with the project. It was given the name of the Moreno Water and Mining Company, the principals consisting of Maxwell, William Kroenig, John Dold, W.H. Moore, Col. V.S. Shelby, M. Bloomfield, and N. S. Davis. Over $200,000 was raised, the bulk of it supplied by Maxwell, and work on the "Big Ditch" got under way in 1868 with Davis in charge of the project.

The Big Ditch began high in the Red River's West Fork canyon at an altitude of about 10,000 feet. It trailed around the ridge, following the natural contour of the mountains, and proceeded to a juncture with the Middlefork Creek where a headgate was located. From here it turned north and then east until it crossed the East Fork from which additional water was drawn. Then the Ditch traversed several miles along the eastern side of the Red River Valley before crossing the ridge at today's Old Red River Pass at a height of 9,852 feet (a drop of about 150 feet from its origin). Here it turned downward into the Moreno watershed and led around the northern end of the valley before turning back south where it emptied into Humbug Gulch near Elizabethtown. In total length the Big Ditch measured slightly more than 41 miles as it followed the mountain contour while the direct distance was only 11 miles. Over three miles of flumes and aqueducts were built where the ditch crossed ravines or worked its way around steep outcroppings of rock. At the various stream crossings headgates were put in place to divert water.

Three of the high mountain lakes were explored and dams were put in place to form reservoirs. At Reservoir #1, known as Snowbound Lake (what is now Horseshoe Lake), a twelve foot dam was put in place. Greatheart Lake (today's Lost Lake) was raised by sixteen feet and designated as Reservoir #2, while a twelve foot dam was built at Pearl Lake (Middlefork Lake) to form Reservoir #3. The initial plans called for a fourth reservoir to be built in Sawmill canyon but for some reason it was never constructed.

GOLD FEVER

Headquarters for the operation was at Ditch Cabin on the East Fork at its juncture with Sawmill Creek.(7) Here several cabins were built and roads for hauling supplies were opened. A water-powered saw mill was constructed and two long ditches were dug to bring water to turn the large waterwheel. For the entire Big Ditch project, over four hundred men were employed, most of whom were miners from E-town. This proved fortuitous since the majority were already experienced in this type of work and all were anxious to complete the job quickly so that water could be provided for their claims in the Moreno Valley. The construction was carried out by hand high on the mountainside using picks, shovels, dynamite, horses, and mules. Most all the flumes, built of wood and mounted on trestles, were 56 inches wide and 30 inches deep. At one location near the top of the Old Red River Pass a long siphon of iron pipe (the Iron Flume) was elevated on a trestle extending 144 rods (2,376 feet) and at one point being elevated 79 feet above the ground. The engineering design anticipated the delivery of 600 miner's inches or about 7.65 million gallons per day.(8)

Amazingly, this entire project was built in less than twelve working months. Construction began on May 28, 1868, was suspended during the winter months because of snow, and the first water reached Humbug Gulch near E-town on July 9, 1869. The story is told that the final bit of construction was completed on July 4 at the top of a canyon which is now called Fourth of July Canyon. At the time, the Big Ditch was considered one of the most remarkable engineering feats in the West.(9)

When water finally flowed into the Moreno Valley there was great disappointment. Due to leakage and seepage, only one-sixth of the anticipated flow was produced, slightly more than one million gallons a day. There was little if any loss in the Red River area but once the water reached the Moreno Valley, it began to seep into the sandy soil underlying the ditch. Although this lost water did not reach the mining area, it entered the underground system

A portion of the Iron Flume showing pipe laid on wooden trestles and several people standing on the pipe
Picture courtesy of the Red River Historical Society

and eventually surfaced in the valley as springs and seeps. For several years the Moreno Creek was the largest tributary of the Cimarron River.

The failure of the Ditch to provide the planned amount of flow meant that there would be insufficient money from the sale of water to maintain the ditch and provide income for the investors. Therefore the major portion of the project was abandoned. The ditch was sold, went through several hands and was eventually purchased by Matthew Lynch in 1875. He instituted repairs and was able to get enough water for his own hydraulic mining operation, while a small surplus was sold to other miners. Lynch operated the ditch for the next five years and during this time it came to be called the Lynch Ditch. Following his untimely death (he suffered the misfor-

GOLD FEVER

tune of standing under a falling tree), his two brothers continued to operate the ditch for another few years after which it fell into disuse.(10)

Despite their disappointment over the failure of the Big Ditch to solve the water problems, the Moreno miners continued to work the claims as best they could. Elizabethtown was still growing and there seemed to be a steady stream of newcomers. At least seventeen different companies were working along Willow Creek and the Michigan Company staked claims in many of the gulches near E-town. Peter Kisinger, Tom Lowthin, and Col. Edward Bergmann worked the Spanish Bar near the mouth of Grouse Gulch and oth-

The Iron Flume. Here the pipe turned upward and emptied water into this wooden flume, 70 feet above the ground. Photo made in 1898.
Picture courtesy of Aultman Studio

A typical wooden flume used to carry water in many places on the Big Ditch.
Picture courtesy of the Museum of New Mexico, #128712

ers spread over the slopes of Baldy into the California and Mexican Gulches. By 1868 the Cimarron Canyon road had been improved and stage service was established between Maxwell's Ranch (Cimarron) and Elizabethtown with a charge of eight dollars for the rough half-day trip. Three sawmills were hard at work turning out lumber for the construction of numerous cabins and buildings so that by the end of the year the *Santa Fe Gazette* was able to report a hundred buildings in the town. The Moreno Hotel went up and not long thereafter, Henry Lambert, who claimed to have been a chef for U.S. Grant, constructed the E-town Hotel. Whatever his boasts, Henry's culinary expertise proved to be true and his restaurant was soon feeding many of the residents. In 1869 the first newspaper appeared, the *Moreno Lantern*. It folded after only a few months and was replaced by the *Elizabethtown Telegraph* with Will Dawson as editor.

Within a couple of years E-town would begin to decline. Although unrecognized at the time, the July 4th celebration of 1871 would mark an end to the boom years. This occasion was marked

GOLD FEVER

with a parade, speeches, picnics, and grand ball which lasted long into the night. The crowds that attended were unaware that soon many of the miners would depart leaving empty homes and buildings. As the richest claims were exhausted and with the ever-present short supply of water, prospectors and miners began to drift. Soon some of the merchants followed and within a few years only about 200 residents remained in Elizabethtown. Henry Lambert moved down to Cimarron and built the famous St. James Hotel, a landmark which operates today. Editor Will Dawson moved to Cimarron where he was hired to operate the *Cimarron News and Press*. An omen and symbol of the future occurred when the county seat was moved from E-town to Cimarron.

For the next fifteen years the search for gold continued though on a rather limited scale. The remaining miners persevered, working their claims and extracting whatever gold could be found. Pros-

The stagecoach station at Elizabethtown, 1896
Picture courtesy of the Museum of New Mexico, #14648

pecting continued, always in the hope that a new and rich lode had been overlooked. Matthew Lynch, who now was in control of the Big Ditch, had enough water to operate his hydraulic system and this yielded modest amounts of gold. E-town, though diminished in numbers, remained busy and fairly stable.

During the 1890s Elizabethtown once again began to boom, largely as a result of fresh discoveries in the surrounding regions. To the north a new gold rush occurred near Comanche Creek in the Valle Vidal area and soon the new mining camp of La Belle would rival E-town in size and population. To the west and just over the ridge lay the Red River Valley which would soon be teeming with hundreds of men caught up in the feverish search for riches. As a result Red River City came into being, a close neighbor but also another rival. Within a short time a large number of newcomers began to wander and explore all the surrounding canyons and the bulk of them came through E-town which was the principal gateway into and out of the mountains. With its road connections to Cimarron and the railroad at Springer, Elizabethtown became a supply and communications center for the new gold rush in northern New Mexico. Soon there was stage service between E-town and La Belle, Red River, and Taos. New merchants came to the town and there was even renewed interest in gold mining in the Moreno Valley.

The town became home to numerous enterprises. There were three hotels, the Moreno Hotel, Mutz Hotel, and the Miner's Inn, operated by John NcIntosh. Froelick's Store along with Remsburg's Store sold general merchandise while Dr. L.L. Cahill operated Cahill's Drug Store. Two butcher shops opened for business, there were several saloons including the Brainard and the Montezuma, and Herman Funk operated the local barber shop.

Around the turn of the century, there was further revival of mining interest at Elizabethtown. It seems that in 1895 a Chicago man by the name of H.J. Reiling had developed the first gold mining dredge in U.S. history. It was put into operation in Montana and was so successful that over the next five years several of these large dredges were built by the Bucyrus Company of Milwaukee. Reiling decided to place a dredge in the E-town area and took an option from the Maxwell Land Grant Company on 258 acres. In February of 1901 he organized the Oro Dredging Company and ordered a dredge which was delivered by rail to Springer. Then began the formidable task of transporting by wagon many loads of heavy machinery (some weighing 20,000 pounds) up the Cimarron Canyon to Elizabethtown. Slowly this was accomplished and by August the giant dredge had been assembled. It was christened the *Eleanor* and was soon at work digging several thousand cubic yards of sand and gravel per day and clearing seven to eight hundred dollars each day in gold. The dredge performed successfully for several years but in 1905 the parent company underwent bankruptcy due to complete failure of its Colorado operations (unrelated to the mining activity at E-town). The result was a suspension of all the company's operations and a public sale of all its assets. Parts of the *Eleanor* were removed and sold as salvage and the remaining structure slowly sank into the sands of the Moreno Valley.

Several of the Moreno Valley's early settlers would come to play a role in the history of Red River and these included the names of Mutz, Gallagher, Lowrey, and Neal. Herman Mutz, who was a German emigrant, came to the Valley in 1881 and later married Tena Storey. Together, they managed the Storey Hotel which had been owned by Tena's parents, Augusta and Chancey Storey. After it was destroyed in the fire of 1903, the hotel was rebuilt, this time of stone, and given the name Mutz Hotel. This large, two-storied structure served as a gathering place for the town and hosted dances, parties, and meetings. Mutz also purchased land near E-town and began a large ranching enterprise which later came to be operated by his sons. Eventually the ranch was divided between several of

The Eleanor, a dredge used at Elizabethtown around 1900 to dig for gold
Picture courtesy of the Red River Historical Society

the Mutz descendants--Robert, Phillip, and Johnny Mutz.

Elizabeth Moore (for whom Elizabethtown was named) grew up to become a school teacher and in 1880 she married Joseph Lowrey. This union produced seven children, four of whom were girls. One of the daughters, Mae Lowrey, would later marry Charles Gallagher whose family had settled in the Moreno Valley (Charles' father, who was originally from Ireland, had come with his wife, Mary, to the Valley during the gold rush and had acquired land near present-day Eagle Nest). Mae and Charles operated a butcher shop in Cimarron for a while but eventually moved back to the ranch in the Valley. They had three sons, Edward, William, and Charles. (11)

A second Lowrey girl, Maude, married T. D. Neal, generally recognized as the founding father of Eagle Nest. Neal, originally from Oklahoma, came to the Moreno Valley in 1919 about the time of completion of Eagle Nest Lake. He purchased land, platted a town site and opened the first store in the new community. He subsequently petitioned for a post office and it was granted under the name of Therma, New Mexico (named for a relative of the postal inspector). This title was never popular with the townspeople and the community later became Eagle Nest. T.D. remained very active in the affairs of the entire Moreno Valley and opened stores in Agua Fria (present-day Angel Fire) as well as in the town of Red River. He also operated a cattle ranch in the upper Red River Valley, a portion of which is still owned by his descendants.

Gradually Elizabethtown began to fade. As the gold production dwindled, many of the miners departed for other mining areas of New Mexico and Colorado. Some of the citizens purchased land and took up ranching while others simply moved away. By 1930 the town was virtually deserted. All that remains today are a few houses, the buildings making up the Elizabethtown Museum, and the stone wall remnants of the Mutz Hotel. The old cemetery sits high on a hill overlooking the Valley and facing Baldy Mountain. Standing here today and gazing down on Humbug and Grouse Gulches, it is easy to imagine how it must have been, with crews of miners scattered over much of the mountainside

The Mutz Hotel in Elizabethtown. Remnants of the structure remain today.
Picture courtesy of the Museum of New Mexico, photo by Hill, #14637

while the noise and bustle of the town echoed across the valley.

La Belle in the Valle Vidal
(1894 - 1905)

The Sangre de Christo Land Grant was originally awarded by Gov. Armijo to the partnership of Narciso Beaubien and Stephen Lee, both of whom were killed in the Taos uprising of 1847. Charles Beaubien inherited half ownership at the death of his son and he quickly bought out the Lee heirs thus assuming full ownership of the grant. Charles lost interest in the property and it was later sold to William Gilpin who had been the first territorial governor of Colorado. After a time Gilpin decided to sell the grant and to make the deal more lucrative he divided it into two parts, the northern Trinchera Estate and the southern Costilla Estate. The Trinchera portion included land that is presently located around Ft. Garland in southern Colorado while the Costilla property encompassed land in New Mexico including the Costilla watershed. A buyer for the Costilla Estate was found in the form of the Dutch banking firm of Werthem and Gompertz, the official sale being consummated in 1870. The new owners quickly organized the United States Freehold Land and Emigration Co. to carry out development of the land. This company was registered in the New Mexico Territory and E.C. Van Diest was appointed manager.

Efforts were made to entice homesteaders and prospectors into the region but with only limited success. A few miners claimed to have found gold but none of these initial prospects proved out. It was not until 1894 that the first serious discovery was made by Ira Wing who staked a claim early that year in the vicinity of Comanche Creek, a tributary of the Costilla and located in the Valle Vidal. When he made his first shipment of gold to Trinidad the word went out and hundreds of miners entered the valley. Although they prospected much of the surrounding area many of them built cabins at the edge of the forest along a small creek flowing eastward into Comanche Creek. By summer there were enough buildings to warrant a townsite which came to be called La Belle, named for Mrs. Belle Dixon, wife of one of the prospectors and one of the few women in the community.

Before year's end the town contained a hundred buildings and over 600 people, including a dozen women and one child. It boasted of a blacksmith shop, two butcher shops, a stable, grocery, hardware and feed store, clothing store, and of course saloons, of which there were three. George Cole built the La Belle Hotel and it soon had a rival, the Chamberlain House. In December, E.W. Iliff began to issue a newspaper, the *La Belle Cresset.*

Meanwhile the excited search for gold went on as miners combed the creeks, canyons, and washes. Ira Wing sold his original claims (the Colorado and Wonder) for $30,000 and set about locating several other prospects. The Golden Jack Milling, Mining and Development Co. of Trinidad hired enough miners to work ten different claims. A Chicago group took an option on the Belle of Mexico while the Climax Mine shipped two thousand pounds of ore to Denver.

Transportation for the isolated community was promptly solved by the building of several roads, some of which were financed by the Freehold Land and Emigration Company. At the time the nearest rail connection was located at Catskill, a small community located 22 miles west of Raton and 45 miles east of La Belle.(12) By the winter of 1894 a road had been opened to Catskill and triweekly stage service established. Soon road connections were made with Elizabethtown, situated only a few miles south and over the mountain ridge. Two roads were built to the west, one following the Cabresto canyon to Questa and the other to Costilla where it connected with the road to Antonito.

Since the La Belle mining district was located on private prop-

The town of La Belle in 1898. The large building is the Southern Hotel.
Picture courtesy of Aultman Studio

erty, miners were required to pay to the Freehold Company a filing fee, a fifty dollar survey charge, and ten dollars per acre for a deed. Some of the men soon realized that by moving a few miles westward to government land they could avoid some of these costs. A few miners traveled over the ridge and came down into the Bitter Creek canyon where they began prospecting. Several strikes were made and the Edison mine was opened along with the nearby Monitor and Denmark. A small settlement of eight cabins were built near the Edison and was given the name of Anchor. A half mile to the west at the headwaters of Cabresto Creek M.K. Long opened the Midnight mine. This attracted other prospectors and numerous claims were filed, including the Raven, Big Stick, Durant, Republican, and Northern Light. Cabins and buildings grew up and the small settlement was given the rather optimistic title of Midnight

City. Within a short time there were several hundred miners working in the region and these men organized the Keystone Mining District which included both the Anchor and Midnight areas. In early 1894 a regular townsite was surveyed at Anchor and seventy lots were sold at public auction (at an average price of $16.00).

The year of 1895 was one of prosperity and optimism for La Belle. By March the town counted 700 citizens and this figure would rise to a thousand by summer. Lots within the townsite were selling for $100 to $350 and new people were arriving daily. By spring new businesses had arrived including several general stores, a drug store, laundry, shoe shop, two barber shops, and a book store; the town could even boast of having its own physician, Dr. W.B. Rice. The Perry Hotel was built and B. Nadoch opened the Exchange Hotel. The largest building project was carried out by Olaf Thomasson who moved the Southern Hotel from Catskill to La Belle. This four-story structure was dismantled, hauled in by wagon, and reconstructed on a prominent site. It was said to contain eighty rooms. The town added three surveyors, a Justice of the Peace, a jail, and to keep pace with prosperity, three new saloons. During the summer, the Freehold Company built a one-room school house and began advertising for a teacher for by this time there were twenty school-age children in the town.

Daily stage service to Catskill and Elizabethtown continued and for a short time there was a scheduled stage route between La Belle and Antonito. Because of the many merchants in town, La Belle began to serve as a supply center for the surrounding area. A variety of trade goods were hauled over the mountain ridge to Anchor and Midnight in the Keystone district. After a road had been built down Bitter Creek, supplies were even sent to the new settlement of Red River City, about twelve miles away.

Although most of the citizens of La Belle worked both long and hard, they also endeavored to maintain a certain level of social and recreational activities. The La Belle Social Club, organized in Au-

The Denmark mine near La Belle
Picture courtesy of Aultman Studio

gust, announced its intention to sponsor Saturday night dances as well as other entertainment including debates and literary discussions. The Club hosted its first annual ball on September 4, a grand event which took place at the Southern Hotel and was attended by many of the townspeople as well as guests from Midnight and Anchor. A five-piece orchestra led the dancing which went through the night and lasted until daylight. The Saturday night dances proved to be popular with the young people and it was not unusual for visitors to come from Elizabethtown, Red River City and Ponil Park.(13) In general these affairs were quite "proper" and although liquor was always present, the heavy drinking took place in saloons and at stag parties. The rule at most of the dance parties was manners, moderation and sobriety. E.W. Iliff, former editor of the *La Belle Cresset*, paid tribute to the young women of La Belle:

GOLD FEVER

"The Trinidad girl
    Is a haughty thing.
If she kisses at all
    Its on the wing.
The Catskill girl
    Is the one to collar
She kisses you good
    For half a dollar.
The E-town girl
    Gives a kiss so sweet
The poets fall down
    At her feet.
There's the Red River girls,

The Aztec mine near La Belle
Picture courtesy of Aultman Studio

> Ah, two for a song.
> Kissing for meal tickets
> All day long.
> But don't forget
>   The girls of La Belle—
> Won't kiss even momma
> For fear she'll tell"

For the men there were baseball games, footraces, boxing and horse races. A baseball team was organized which played against teams from the surrounding towns of Catskill, Elizabethtown, Midnight, and Trinidad. Horse races were held among the locals and later challenges were sent out to the neighboring communities. Also, a men's group, the Limeklin Club, was organized to provide entertainment during the long evening hours. In addition to these more respectable and proper activities, the saloons were often filled, resulting in the usual drunkenness and brawls. Like all the gold camps, La Belle had its red light district which everyone recognized but no one talked about.

During the year of 1896 there began a subtle shift in the mood of the miners of La Belle. Although modest amounts of gold were still being found it seemed clear to all that in spite of two years of hard work, no rich vein, no bonanza had been uncovered. The ore was inconsistent and low grade, so much so that many tons of rock had to be dug in order to produce significant amounts of gold. The effort and cost of moving this much ore the forty-five miles to the railroad at Catskill largely offset whatever profit might be expected. Gradually pessimism and disappointment set in and miners began to leave the valley. By the end of the year the numbers in the town had dropped to about 800 and the following year to 500. This was only a prelude to the exodus that would soon follow.

While the fortunes of La Belle declined, the Keystone district continued to boom. A rich strike took place at the Edison mine at

GOLD FEVER 71

Anchor and there was renewed activity around the community of Midnight. At the Midnight mine the shaft had reached a depth of 175 feet and the Ohio group which had leased the property was working a crew of fifteen men. The town of Midnight was still growing and by 1897 had surpassed Anchor in population. Many cabins were built, and a hotel as well as was a boarding house opened up. A new road over the mountain was constructed making travel to La Belle and Catskill quicker and easier. However, all the enthusiasm would be short-lived as the district began to undergo the same problems as its neighbors. Uneven and spotty ore, along with the usual transportation problems, soon would prove to be too much for the Keystone district.

Remains of the hotel at Midnight. Photo made about 1925.
Picture courtesy of the Red River Historical Society

Over the next couple of years the entire region continued to decline at an ever-increasing rate. As capital for operating the mines slowly dried up, many of the miners and prospectors departed and not long after the merchants followed. Hotels and saloons closed down and finally even the *La Belle Cresset* had to close its doors. In 1900 the drugstore in La Belle moved to E-town, for by then only 50 residents remained. At the end of the same year only six people still lived in Midnight and Anchor had become a ghost town. Soon La Belle itself would be vacant.

Today nothing remains of La Belle. The old stage road can still be found and there are a few remains of cabins along Gold Creek and near the trail that leads to Anchor. There is only a hunting lodge to mark the site of the old town, situated along La Belle Creek and looking over the beautiful Valle Vidal. Standing at this place today it is hard to visualize the once bustling town with its throngs of people, alive with their joys and laughter, hopes and dreams.(14)

RED RIVER CITY
(1890 -1920)

The town of Red River was founded in 1895, the last of the four gold camps to be settled and the only one to survive. The fact that it was late in coming was due in large part to the relative isolation of the Red River Valley. Yet it remains somewhat of a mystery why the area did not draw prospectors sooner, especially during the E-town boom of the late 1860s. At that time the Big Ditch was built and several hundred workers wandered much of the Upper Valley. Many of these men were miners from the Moreno Valley and they must have realized the gold potential, but as far as we know, there were no claims staked in the Red River region at that time. It is possible that these miners already had proven claims around Elizabethtown and were simply anxious to complete their job on the Ditch and get back to working these prospects.

During the 1890s there was renewed gold fever in much of northern New Mexico and an influx of many new people. Along the Rio Hondo at Twining new mines were opened and near Comanche Creek the town of La Belle was bursting with new growth and enthusiasm. Even Elizabethtown, now twenty years old, seemed to be undergoing a renewal. It was only natural that some of the many gold-seekers would drift over the mountain ridges and into the Red River Valley so that by the time of the town's founding the Red River area contained about two hundred people. Soon roads would be opened and before long stage and mail service would be established between the various communities. As a result, newcomers continued to pour into the valley and Red River City would soon outnumber its older neighbors.

As the town grew, prospectors searched and explored all the tributaries of the Red River and left their mark in almost all the canyons. However the bulk of the active mining took place along four streams: Pioneer, Bitter Creek, Placer, and Black Copper. It was here that the major strikes were made and here was located the large mining and milling operations.

The Red River Valley enjoyed one advantage not held by two of its neighboring towns. Both E-town and La Belle happened to be situated on land that was privately owned, one by the Maxwell Land Grant Company and the other by the Freehold Land and Emigration Company. Any property located here had to be purchased from the owners. On the other hand, the Red River area was situated on government land and thus was open to homesteading. As a result, along with the large number of miners and prospectors who were mostly single, the town began to see an increased numbers of permanent settlers and families. This had the effect of providing more permanency to the town and there would soon appear those family names which would provide future generations to Red River: Mallette, Young, Brandenburg, Oldham, Phipps, Hatton, etc.

As the 20th century opened, the great gold rush of northern New Mexico began to fade. A few mines continued to be worked and the feverish optimism would only die slowly, but there was a slow exodus from all the camps. The old difficulties of uneven ore quality, insufficient capital, and transportation problems could not be overcome. La Belle became deserted, Twining would soon empty, and Elizabethtown found itself in a steady decline. Red River City hung on even though it too faced a doubtful future; it certainly seemed that it would follow its neighbors and become another ghost town. And then a strange thing happened. Newcomers began to appear, visitors not in search of gold, but come to see the natural beauty, fish the streams, and enjoy the mountain climate. They did not stay long but seemed to return again and again. Not many at first but their numbers slowly increased. It just might be that the old mining town would live on but now in a different way.

In 1879 a trio of prospectors consisting of D.W. Stevens and the

Terhune brothers, William and Garrett, struck gold near the present-day town of Red River. They organized as the Red River Mining Company and obtained outside capital from a group of Chicago men associated with the Waterbury Watch Company. Extensive working of the claim yielded only low-grade ore and all efforts were eventually suspended. Four years later Warren White came to the Valley and after exploring along the river, decided to open operations. He organized the Pioneer Mining Company and filed three claims near the mouth of Pioneer Creek as well as other claims further down the Red River Canyon. After two years of hard work with little to show he gave up further efforts. In 1885 attempts were made to revive the old Waterbury Watch Co. mine after further prospecting revealed the presence of fairly large amounts of copper. It was decided to attempt to treat the ore at the mine so as to avoid the heavy transportation costs of moving it. Money was raised, a smelter was ordered, shipped in, and preparations were made. After several runs of ore were carried out it became apparent that the production would hardly meet expenses, so the project was abandoned.

Although this activity created interest and resulted in various prospecting, gradually the miners drifted to other areas and the Valley became empty. It was not until six years later that two men, Phillip Lama and Joseph Hamilton, spent a summer prospecting and exploring. They returned the following year accompanied by Sylvester (Vet) Mallette, a friend from Ft. Garland. Mallette fell in love with the beauty of the Valley and the following year, 1893, he brought his brothers, Orrin and George. Only partly interested in prospecting, they came primarily to homestead, settling with their families on a permanent basis. By planting a few crops, catching fish, and hunting game, the Mallettes were able to subsist in their new home.(1) The next year brought others including three trappers, Ed Westoby, Charles Compton, and William Sellers and not long after men wandered in from La Belle such as Jarrret Moad and Thomas Melson.

By 1895 the valley began to swarm with miners and settlers who scattered over the valley, along Bitter Creek and into Pioneer Canyon. By summer there were more than two hundred people in the beautiful Red River Valley.

Orrin Mallette and his wife Julia built a cabin in the western part of the Valley and filed claim on 96 acres listed as the Willow Placer Mining Claim. Here they raised their two children, Roy and Ethel. In addition to farming and prospecting, Orrin operated a blacksmith shop as well as a brick kiln (the bricks, pinkish in color, were mainly used in building chimneys).

Sylvester Mallette, a lifelong bachelor, raised a cabin in the eastern part of town but it subsequently had to be moved since its location was part of the original Red River City plat. The third brother, George, along with his wife Mary Emma, built their home near the head of Bobcat Canyon, and all four of their children were born there. They owned a dairy cow and Emma would ride down the canyon on horseback to deliver milk to the customers in town.

Like all the gold camps Red River had its share of schemers, promoters, and deal-makers. One such was a man named E.I. Jones who arrived from Colorado in 1895. Estimating that more profit could be made from selling land than could be acquired in mining claims, he decided to develop a townsite. Somehow Jones was able to convince the Mallettes that part of the land upon which they were homesteading could only be proved up as a mining claim and he was able to buy them out for a small sum of money. Acquiring other claims he consolidated all his property as the Gilt Edge Placer Claim and then formed the Red River City Town and Mineral Company. A townsite was laid out on the Gilt Edge claim and lots were advertised for sale.

Since Jones had not yet received a patent (and thus a title) on the land he could not legally give deeds to the buyers so they were issued a title bond with the promise that deeds would be available within ninety days. Lots were sold but as time passed Jones had

RED RIVER CITY

still not received a patent on the property and no deeds were forthcoming. This aroused scepticism among the townspeople who began to question the validity of the scheme and whether the company's rights were legal. Some even went so far as to begin settling on some of the lots as if they represented unowned land. Subsequently, a meeting of the townspeople was held setting a deadline date for the deeds to be issued, and in the meantime Jones had appealed to the county sheriff to begin evicting those who had seized lots without payment. Tempers flared on both sides and threats were made against Jones. The citizens then appealed to the sheriff, claiming that Jones had acquired their money under false pretenses. As a result Jones was arrested but the case was promptly dismissed. All of this led to a meeting of the townspeople at which time they

Orrin Mallette's wheat field, located in the western end of the Red River Valley
Picture courtesy of the Red River Historical Society

The George Mallette farm located at the top of Bobcat Pass
Picture courtesy of the Red River Historical Society

elected their own officials: Paul Baca became Justice of the Peace, J.M. Phipps the new deputy sheriff, and Sylvester Mallette to serve as the road overseer.

It was more than a year before the U.S. Land Office awarded Jones the patent (and therefore title) on the Gilt Edge Placer property but at last he was able to issue deeds. Some of the original squatters still remained on portions of the property and Jones obtained injunctions against them. The old animosity against him resurfaced and reached such a point that Jones was forced to leave the area and return to Colorado, leaving a local agent to operate the company. Eventually all the disagreements were settled between the parties and the settlers received proper legal title to their land.

While these conflicts over land titles went on, there was a steady stream of new prospectors into the Valley and the town of Red River City continued to grow. By 1897 there were 250 permanent residents as well as numerous miners scattered in tents and cabins throughout the adjacent canyons. New buildings and cabins went up at a furious pace, especially after a sawmill was put in operation by B.J. Young, one of the new arrivals, and one whose name would be influential in the life of Red River.

Brigham J. Young (said to be related to and named for the original Brigham Young) was born in Virginia but his family migrated westward and he grew up in Fairview, Utah. There he married Sara Elizabeth Wilson in 1882 and the Youngs subsequently moved to Colorado. By the time of their arrival in Red River City in 1895 the family included seven children. Young not only turned out lumber from his sawmill but he also operated a mercantile store, in addition to holding positions as Justice of the Peace and as the first postmaster. He and Sara (Lizzie) would produce six more children, giving them a grand total of thirteen youngsters and this large family gave a considerable boost to the future student body of the Red River school. The Youngs built a home in the middle of town on what is now Main Street, their house being the only brick dwelling in the entire town (the bricks were produced in the kiln on Orin Mallette's property). For the next hundred years four generations of Youngs would contribute to the life of the town.(2)

Other merchants and businessmen built a variety of establishments. L.F. Butler opened his Jayhawk store, J.J. Justice operated a livery and Gerson Gusdorf from Taos built a mercantile store. Soon there were three hotels--the Victoria, the Clare, and the Pioneer. Ed Brailey and C.G. Cleland served as blacksmiths and R.A. Strain opened an assay office. Two partners named Morris and Thompson operated the Red River Grocery and there were, of course, a good many saloons to serve the prospectors and miners who continued to appear in the Valley. The first butcher shop was opened by a man named Brandenburg and as things turned out he and his descendents would play a large role in the subsequent history of Red River.

Harry N. Brandenburg was born in 1852 in Illinois where his father was engaged in the sale of meat products. He later married Margaret Hilton of Chicago and the young couple moved to El Moro, Colorado, a small town near Trinidad. It was in Colorado that three children were born--John F. (Jack), Charles, and Charlotte. News of the gold rush in northern New Mexico prompted Harry and Margaret to move to Red River City, where they arrived in 1895. They established the first meat market in the new town and it continued to operate for nearly twenty years. Harry served for a time as Justice of the Peace and, like most of the local citizens, dabbled in gold mining; at one time he was part owner of the well-known Black Copper mine. However, most of his interests remained in the meat business and during one period he operated a second shop in Taos. Throughout his life, Harry Brandenburg remained a leading figure in the story of Red River and both he and Margaret are buried in the Red River Cemetery.(3)

B. J. and Sara Young with their large family
Picture courtesy of the Red River Historical Society

RED RIVER CITY

The Young house on Main Street, the only brick home in the town
Picture courtesy of the Red River Historical Society

A pressing need for the new community was the establishing of better roads and communications with the surrounding towns. As a first step, a rather crude road was built down the Red River canyon to Questa, thus opening the way to Taos and Santa Fe. By far the most important traffic access was eastward to Elizabethtown (and thereby to the railroad at Springer) so a road was quickly constructed over the mountain ridge, down the "Big Hill", and through Road Canyon. This road was rather daunting with a very steep grade of 27 degrees in some places. It became common practice to chain a log to the back of the wagons and apply full brakes in order to control the descent; at times heavily loaded wagons had to be let down by ropes. A journey down the Big Hill provided many a new visitor with an exciting introduction to the town of Red River. This road remained the only eastward access for nearly twenty years until a new Pass Road was built by the Forest Service.(4)

Another road was soon opened up Bitter Creek Canyon, thus connecting the Red River Valley with the mining communities of Anchor and Midnight, and therefore access to La Belle. By 1897 both stage and mail service had been established between Red River City and Elizabethtown, La Belle, Ft. Garland, Cimarron, and Catskill.

Early efforts to serve the town with a newspaper were not very successful. The *Review,* edited by O.D. Crain and the *Record,* put out by C.W. Morgan, were short-lived. Later, George P. Beringer published a weekly called the *Mining News* which survived for four years. In 1899, Fremont Stevens began the Red River *Prospector* which would serve the town for slightly more than eight years. This weekly paper carried some national news, a great deal about local happenings, and the usual amount of gossip (the yearly subscription rate was $1.50).

Within a year after the town's founding, the citizens decided to build a school for the growing number of children. Money was

Red River City in the early 1900s
Picture courtesy of the Red River Historical Society

raised and a log school house was built on High Street. Mrs. Ida Phipps was appointed the first teacher and the number of students stood at between twenty and thirty. For a number of years the building served not only as a school house but also as a place for town meetings, church services, and a variety of social events. This building remained for nearly twenty years when it came to be replaced by the Little Red School House.(5)

This growth and prosperity in Red River City was fueled by the furious search for gold and the continuing arrival of gold seekers into the valley. The new mining industry included a variety of different activities and involved many and diverse people. At the most basic level were those attempting to locate the gold--prospectors and miners--most of whom were single and often loners, though occasionally working in twos or threes. They would search a variety of places until locating what seemed to be a promising source, then file a claim and subsequently work the claim to substantiate the amount and value of the minerals. If such a claim proved to be successful and promising it would then be sold to a developer. The prospector would move on, searching for other claims, or even might move to another area. It was not at all unusual for miners and prospectors to wander back and forth between the various gold camps depending upon which seemed to be the most active and lucrative.

The mining developer would try to form an organization, which might purchase several adjacent proven mining claims, in the hope that a working mine might be organized. Since this required a certain amount of money, most of the developers were forced to take on several partners. It was commonplace for settlers and business people of Red River to become part owners and investors in these mining ventures even though they, themselves, were not miners or prospectors. Many of them had other sources of income which provided the investment money.

Once a promising group of claims had been purchased and

The Jayhawk Store in early Red River City
Picture courtesy of the Red River Historical Society

organized, the next task was to raise sufficient capital for the actual mine operation (usually a large sum of money was required). In the late 1900s there was almost no venture capital in the New Mexico Territory so this meant a search of financial markets in such cities as St. Louis, Chicago, Denver, New York, or Philadelphia. A mining company, or syndicate, would be formed, stock sold to moneyed investors, and if sufficient funds were accumulated, an operating mine would be undertaken. The necessary heavy equipment would be ordered and arrangements made for delivery by rail and then by wagon. Next, miners would be hired to dig shafts and tunnels, remove the ore and bring it to the surface. After the ore had received initial treatment in a mill, it had to be sent to the smelter at Denver (later, Colorado Springs). Only after the smelting was there any actual return on the original investment. Major difficulties at any of the series of steps might cause the entire venture to fail. However, in

Typical steam boiler and winch used to drive the cables reaching down into a mine shaft
Picture courtesy of the Red River Historical Society

spite of the many problems and uncertainties, most of those seeking their fortune remained optimistic and expected to hit the great bonanza.

In Pioneer Canyon the Mallette brothers worked their Ajax claim but eventually sold out to a group of Denver investors. In the same area D.B. Hayes worked a tunnel and the Tom Thumb claims were developed by C.G. Cleland. William Baxter operated the Last Chance mine which was later named the Stella by B.J. Young and came to be operated by the Red River Mining Company. Further up the canyon a Trinidad syndicate organized as the Black Mountain Mining Company had opened the Inferno and tunneled nearly a thousand feet into the mountain. Within a short time a wagon road had been extended seven miles up Pioneer and much of the canyon had been explored.(6)

Meanwhile, several claims were filed in Mallette Canyon and B.J. Young worked the I.X.L. in Bobcat Canyon. Located in Road Canyon was the Ragged Pants Dick Mine. Ed Westoby developed a claim not far from his cabin near the east end of the town of Red River and in partnership with Al Hedges worked the Willard, a mile south of town.(7) Up Bittercreek toward Anchor and Midnight there was a great deal of exploration, especially after completion of the road through this canyon. Ed Hatton developed the June Bug, while R.L. Pooler worked the Memphis properties, and a variety of other claims were being explored. Further up the canyon at Anchor the Edison Mine had produced a rich strike and around Midnight there was renewed activity.

The most exciting finds took place south of town along Placer Creek and in Black Copper Canyon. Up Placer Canyon several claims were purchased by a Trinidad group organized as the Jayhawk Gold Mining and Milling Company. They opened the Jayhawk Mine and soon reached a depth of 300 feet. Assays showed more than eighty dollars per ton in gold. Nearby, the Blue Rock tunnel was developed by R.P. and John Kelly. This claim was later acquired by the Buffalo New Mexico Mines Company, a group headquartered in Buffalo, New York. After the main shaft of the Buffalo became flooded, a new tunnel was dug in the vicinity to drain the water. Also in the area Charles Compton worked his Silver King.

The most promising mine in this location was opened by the Oldham brothers--Read, Rich, and George. Along with two other brothers, they had been brought west from Missouri in 1874 by their father, Richard Oldham. It was actually his second trip to New Mexico since he had served in the Army of the West, the force led by General Kearny which had invaded the Territory in 1846 during the Mexican-American war. The Oldham family settled in Trinidad and later in Raton. There all five of the brothers had engaged in a variety of work: as ranch hands and cowboys, as railhands on the M.R. & G.L. Railroad, and as operators of a livery stable. Read, Rich, and George came to Red River in 1895 as part of the gold rush and quickly began to explore the upper forks of Placer Creek. They opened the Golden Treasure and Golden Calf mines after discovery

Remains of the old smelter, located at the site of today's main chair lift on Pioneer Road
Picture courtesy of the Red River Historical Society

ore was assayed at two thousand dollars a ton. Several buildings were constructed in the area including the Oldham cabin, shaft houses and the beginnings of an assay office. George Oldham drew the plans for, and the brothers constructed, a large water wheel to power an arrastra which was used to crush the ore. In order to turn the wheel, water was brought to the site in a mile-long ditch originating in Goose Creek. (This was one of three water wheels which the Oldhams built in the Red River area.) Unfortunately, just as the Golden Treasure was becoming productive, it flooded and the brothers had difficulty in completely clearing the water.(8)

Not far away were a series of claims developed by James O. Gill. The Oldham brothers, along with several others, became partners in developing these as the Bunker Hill Mine. This mine seemed to have great promise and although much effort was spent developing it, the property never lived up to expectations. James O.

Remains of the Edison mine located at Anchor on Bitter Creek
Picture courtesy of the Red River Historical Society

Gill and his son Tom prospected in the upper Placer canyon as well as along Goose Creek.(9)

Through the efforts of Ed Hatton a toll road was built from the Placer Creek area directly over the mountain to the mouth of Pioneer Canyon. This would provide a shorter route for shipping ore to the smelter which was being planned.(10)

Four miles up the canyon from the town of Red River lies Black Copper Creek and here in 1896 Neal and H.C. Garner filed claim on land that would become the Black Copper Mine. They took in a partner, Harry Brandenburg, and hired several miners to work the property. The following spring there was a major strike with ore supposedly assaying at a hundred thousand dollars a ton. This immediately set off a flurry of activity throughout the Upper Valley and prospectors flooded the area. The Black Copper Mining District was formed and efforts began to open a road between E-town and

The Oldham assay house at the Golden Treasure mine, never completed and called the "Unfinished Cabin"
Picture courtesy of the J. R. Pierce collection

the Black Copper. Through cooperative efforts a road was extended from Elizabethtown up Hematite Creek to the community of Hematite, thence to the ridge and down Fourth of July Canyon. At the valley floor it ran south and the entered Black Copper Canyon.

In order to provide a means of treating what was expected to be a large production of ore, the Franklin Placer Company began building sluices to serve the ever-increasing number of miners. These sluices were located near the junction of Fourth of July Creek and the Red River. The company built several cabins nearby for its workers and this collection of buildings was given the rather pretentious title of Franklin City.

Active exploration at the Black Copper Mine continued and soon there were more than fifty men working in the District. Then, for reasons which are not clear, there occurred an abrupt and significant change in ownership of the Black Copper. The Garners bought out Brandenburg and accepted a new partner, A.T. Gunnell of Colorado. Subsequently, quarrels between the new ownership and the mine operators broke out, resulting in a major curtailment of the mine operation. By summer, only six men remained on the payroll.

By the following year all disagreements had been resolved, full production was resumed, and 24 men were back at work. It was decided to build a stamp mill at the Black Copper in order to crush the ore on site. Machinery was ordered from Denver and it was delivered and put in place in early 1901.(11) Once again, for reasons that are not clear, there was a sudden slow down in work at the

The Oldham water wheel at the Golden Treasure mine
Picture courtesy of the Red River Historical Society

mine and a year later it had been closed completely. Several reasons have been offered for the failure of so promising a mine as the Black Copper: arguments between owners, litigation over ownership, difficulty in shipping the ore, lack of operating capital, or possibly all of these. One might suspect that the major problem was simply a lack of money. Curtailment of activity at the Black Copper had a chilling effect throughout the area and spelled doom to Franklin City.

There were other disappointments in the Red River Mining District. A major problem for the mining companies was the difficulty and cost of moving ore to smelters in Colorado. In an effort to alleviate this, the Red River Mining Company decided to erect a smelter for its own use as well as the other mines in the area. The proper machinery was ordered from St. Louis and construction of the necessary housing and buildings was begun. Ore was stockpiled

Remains of the Oldham cabin at the Golden Treasure
Picture courtesy of the J. R. Pierce collection

at the various mines and by early 1898 all seemed ready. Unfortunately, as often happened in the mining camps, those in charge knew very little about the actual operation of a smelter (at the time, the processing and smelting of gold ore was a complex and tedious procedure which required considerable experience; simply acquiring the machinery was hardly sufficient). On the first run the ore "froze" and formed a solid precipitate in the machinery which had to be chipped out by hand using picks. After this had been completed, a second run was begun. This time water was inadvertently turned on the hot boiler resulting in an explosion. Several men were injured including Harry Brandenburg. As a result the operation was suspended while new machinery was ordered and shipped. After several months, all seemed ready again and another trial run was begun. The ore promptly froze again, necessitating the removal of the solid material with picks. Once this long and tedious job was completed, another run took place only to result in the ore freezing again. Amid great

Remains of the Stamp Mill at the Black Copper Mine, built in 1901. Picture made in 1997.
Picture courtesy of the J. R. Pierce collection

disappointment all operations ceased and the smelting works were abandoned.(12)

About this same time efforts were underway to develop a custom mill for the entire Red River Valley--a mill to crush, treat, and concentrate the ore being dug from various mines. The original idea came from Ed Hatton, manager of the June Bug Mine on Bitter Creek. He was able to convince his Waco, Texas backers (led by Dr. H.W. Brown and his son, R. Brown) to undertake such a venture and work began in 1899. The proper machinery was ordered and while awaiting its delivery, the housing for the mill was built as quickly as possible. In fact, on several occasions B.J. Young's sawmill could hardly keep up with the construction. Finally, the machinery arrived and its installation began. All of this activity inspired the miners to work harder at their claims and to increase production. Stockpiling of large amounts of ore was carried out. At the Memphis Mine alone, 300 tons of ore was gathered, awaiting the new mill's production. By June, 1901 the June Bug mill was completed and ready for work. The first runs produced satisfactory yields but subsequent runs resulted in only small amounts of gold. In July a fire broke out in the works requiring a shutdown in production. Some machinery had to be replaced and efforts were made to somehow increase the efficiency of the process. Finally, the mill operation began once more, but the yields remained disappointingly low. In fact, the yields were so low as to be almost worthless. Once again it became apparent that the mill operators did not have enough knowledge to operate the machinery and carry out the milling process.(13)

Despite these setbacks the people of Red River City remained optimistic. Newcomers continued to arrive in the town and were welcomed with enthusiasm. New merchants were arriving including J.P. Phipps, George Walters, W.J. Cartwright, and Ed Halton. The Jayhawk store was purchased by the Abbott brothers, then expanded and enlarged. Louis Macarti opened a dry goods store and George

Mallette expanded his dairy business. John Williams moved his saloon from Elizabethtown; it, along with the other saloons, experienced a thriving business.

The townspeople continued to find time for leisure activities and social events. Dances, balls, and parties were popular and held on a regular basis. These took place in various business establishments or in the school house. Vet Mallette would play his violin accompanied by Jesse Young on the piano and dancing would last until midnight. Then there would be a break for supper, giving all a rest so the dancing could be continued till dawn. Social entertaining between the several gold camps became popular and the young people would often travel to E-town, La Belle or Midnight for an evening of entertainment. The Fourth of July celebration was always a major event and in 1899 the newspaper reported, "Red River had a fine time on the Fourth of July. There was singing, music, and speaking, also races of all kinds. Little Joe Phipps carried off the prize in the boys race and Bessie Phipps won the girls race. Coke, lemonade, and ice cream was free to all. A dance in the evening was enjoyed by all present."

As the 20th century opened, the overall mood of the community began a subtle and as yet hardly recognized change. In spite of an apparent influx of newcomers, as many people were leaving the town as arriving. New businesses were going up but others were closing. According to the Taos *Cresset* the Red River population in 1901 was down to 201 citizens and the school enrollment that year was 22 students. Although miners and prospectors seemed busy throughout the District, no one appeared to be making much money and in spite of over six years of exploration there was still no great bonanza. The community was beginning to come up against the same problems that had beset the other gold towns.

The ore was very inconsistent in its content. There were rich pockets but many of these were small so that further digging in the same area might produce very little gold or silver. As a result, miners

RED RIVER CITY

had to produce many tons of ore to yield a significant return of money. A second problem was the ever-present shortage of capital. The proper organization and operation of a gold mine is not only an expensive investment but also a risky one. There are many steps and oftentimes many delays between the initial up-front money and the ultimate gold production at the smelter. The type of risk capital required was not available in the New Mexico Territory and investors had to be found in the money centers of the Eastern United States. As a result of these factors, the New Mexico mines were poorly funded and chronically short of money; the slightest mishap could result in financial ruin.

Then there was the persistent problem of transporting ore out of the mountains to the smelters in Colorado. In spite of a variety of efforts, there was still no close railroad connection. The Santa Fe Railroad served Springer and eventually the tracks were extended to Cimarron and further to Ute Park to serve the Aztec mine on the east side of Baldy mountain. Plans to lay track into the Moreno Valley never materialized and in any event this came too late for the Red River mines. To the west the nearest connections were at Antonito and Jaroso, Colorado, too far to be of much benefit to the Valley miners. As a result, the ore was hauled by wagon over long and difficult roads resulting in transportation costs that were prohibitive.(14) Efforts to get around the transportation problems by erecting local mills and smelters had proven fruitless.

A general mood of pessimism began to spread among the citizens and there was a gradual and increasing exodus from the Valley. Prospectors and miners began to leave and not long thereafter, merchants and businessmen followed. Even B.J. Young left for Colorado, taking most of his family with him (Jesse Young remained behind, and as we shall see, played a major role in the revival of Red River City). This decline in the fortunes of the town was matched by similar events in the surrounding communities. Midnight and Anchor were virtually deserted and La Belle contained only a few people. Twining was rapidly dwindling and even Elizabethtown was on a rapid downhill course. Finally, events reached a low point in 1908 when a major fire broke out destroying much of the town, including several large buildings, the newspaper office, a blacksmith shop, office building, and a saloon.

Around 1910, in a surprising turn of events, there was a sudden renewed interest and enthusiasm for the Red River mines. Once again prospectors roamed the canyons looking for new strikes as well as attempting to reexamine the old claims. A new group of mine operators and investors appeared and the town began to grow and prosper once again.

There were several reasons for this renaissance in the mining industry, and some of them were related to technological advances which had come about around the turn of the century. Newer and more efficient methods of crushing the ore had been invented. The

Red River City around 1920. Buildings in the center are Clapper's Grandview Camp and Store. The road to the right is High Street and the store faces today's JayHawk Trail.
Picture courtesy of the Red River Historical Society

older devices such as the arrastra and stamp mill were heavy, cumbersome, and difficult to put in place. Now, there were small ore crushers which could be operated and transported more easily. Ball mills (15) had come into use and these could grind the ore to the optimum size. The greatest advance was development of a new cyanide process for separating gold from the ore. This was much more efficient than the previous milling devices and smelters and allowed for much greater yield from a given amount of ore. The process was much easier to perform so that final milling could be carried out at the mine without great expertise.

In addition, the overall economy, both in New Mexico and the country at large had improved. As a result, investment capital was not quite as scarce, though still difficult to obtain. Transportation

A water wheel shown on the left driving an arrastra on the right, the latter a device used to crush the ore. The man on the right is said to be Ed Westoby.
Picture courtesy of the Red River Historical Society

into and out of the gold fields was still a major problem though there were indications this might improve. The railroads were no closer but the local roads were improved. In 1913 a new road from Red River to Questa was built and two years later the Forest Service built the new road over the Red River Pass. Besides, motor vehicles began to appear and although these early trucks were somewhat crude they were a marked improvement over the horse drawn wagons.

Then there was the human factor. Fresh, eager, and hard-working prospectors were able to uncover newer and better sources of gold and silver. Old claims were carefully reexamined and tunnels and shafts were extended.

Bitter Creek Canyon was one of the first areas of renewed activity after John Lachaniche and Louis Marchino filed on the Independence claims located a few miles above Red River City. When their ore was assayed at $10,000 a ton, this set off a new round of enthusiasm for the Bitter Creek region--prospectors flocked to the area, and new claims and mines were opened. Lachaniche and Marchino were able to obtain financing and opened the Independence Mine. They set about building cabins, a bunkhouse, an assay shop, and they ordered two steam boilers, an air compressor and new air drills.

About the time when all was ready for the mine to begin production there was a major legal snag. The question was raised as to the exact siting of the Independence and whether it was actually located on the Costilla Estate of the Sangre de Christo Land Grant. This section of land was privately owned by the U.S. Freehold Land and Emigration Company(16) and as such was subject to special rules regarding filing of claims and mine ownership. A legal patent (title) on the property could not be obtained until the question of location was settled. The mine owners suspended all work and hired a U.S. government surveyor to settle the question. This survey declared the Independence to be on government land and outside the Sangre de Christo Grant. However, The Freehold Company refused to accept this, questioned the survey, and filed suit in court. After many months this was eventually settled in favor of the Independence owners, but during the long delay they expended all their funds and exhausted their resources. As a result, the two owners were forced to sell a controlling interest to William R. Powell of Philadelphia. With the infusion of more capital, work went forward and at one time there were twenty-four miners at work. The company shipped several loads of ore but the return was only fair. Gradually the rich pocket of ore played out and there was threat of further litigation. The Independence was eventually abandoned.

Further down Bitter Creek, William Kershner and R.L."Grandpa" Pooler reworked the Memphis Mine and in 1913 discovered a vein of rich ore. They incorporated as the Memphis-Red River Mining Company and were able to raise $300,000 from a group of St.

Louis Scarvarda at his Neptune mine on Bitter Creek
Picture courtesy of the Red River Historical Society

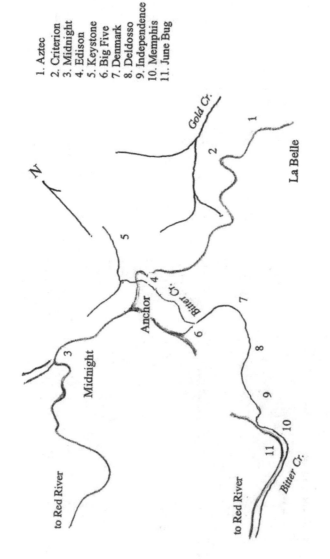

ANCHOR MINING SUBDISTRICT - La Belle, Anchor, Midnight, Bitter Cr.

1. Aztec
2. Criterion
3. Midnight
4. Edison
5. Keystone
6. Big Five
7. Denmark
8. Deldosso
9. Independence
10. Memphis
11. June Bug

RED RIVER CITY

Louis and Kansas City backers. A couple of years earlier the June Bug Mill had been bought by the Trinidad Mining and Milling Co. which had installed a cyanide process. Sixty tons of ore from the Memphis was treated at the new June Bug and yielded thirty dollars per ton. Thusly encouraged, Kershner and Pooler hired extra miners and began to stockpile ore. They decided to install their own mill and this was completed in 1916. The initial runs seemed very successful with a high yield from the ore. However, by the following year the returns were disappointing and they continued to diminish. Two years later the mill was leased to the R and S Molybdenum Company and all work in the tunnels was stopped.

On the west side of Bitter Creek and opposite the Memphis, Louis Scarvarda purchased three claims, the Neptune, Morning Star, and Varida. He lived in Colorado where he owned a general store, packing house and a ranch. At the Neptune he built a cabin

Remains of a cabin at the Independence Mine on Bitter Creek
Picture courtesy of the J. R. Pierce collection

and spent most of his summers working the claims. Nothing of much value was ever produced. On one occasion two car loads of ore were shipped to El Paso but the net was only $65.00. In 1928 the work was turned over to his son, Charlie Scarvarda.(17)

A half mile above the Independence Mine, Pete Deldosso worked his claim and further up the canyon the Orofino (Big Five) was developed by C.C. Lowe. He built a cabin, installed a small mill, a water wheel, and a steam boiler and steam engine.(18) At the town of Anchor, the Edison Mine was reworked by the Edison Mining and Milling Company. A ten-stamp mill was installed, powered by a steam engine. For a brief time ore was recovered yielding $14.00 a ton but this did not hold out for long. The Edison was located only a few feet above the stream and water in the mine was always a problem.

During this same period there was also renewed work in Placer Canyon. The old Blue Rock Tunnel and the Silver King group (first located around 1900) were taken over by the Buffalo-New Mexico Mining Company in 1910. This company was headquartered in Buffalo, New York and initially was well financed. John J. Kelly was appointed superintendent and the company installed a bunkhouse, cookhouse, boiler, steam hoist, air compressor, and a saw mill. Ore was treated at the June Bug Mill, which now had a cyanide process, and the yield showed $12.50 per ton. At one time water filled the mine, so a second shaft was dug in order to drain the tunnel. The Buffalo remained fairly profitable for several years but work was suspended during World War I. After the war the mine was reopened and was operated off and on for several more years. During its lifetime the Buffalo Mine employed a number of miners and the list included Harry and Lorrain Young, Jack Brandenburg, Bert Phipps, Gilbert and Earl Fuller, and Jesse Young.

Further up the West Fork of Placer Creek, the Jayhawk Mine had been put back in operation by the Jayhawk Gold Mining and Milling Company. With new financing the mine was refurbished with a new boiler, ore crusher, and a concentrating mill. A new shaft was drilled down fifty feet and the tunnel extended. The Placer road was improved to make access to the mine much easier. In spite of all these efforts the Jayhawk was never very successful and in 1910 the mine was acquired by the Caribel Milling and Mining Company.

Still further up Placer the Oldhams continued to work the Golden Treasure and the Golden Calf. Their yield of gold was not spectacular but steady and water in the tunnels seemed almost a continuous problem. Nevertheless, the brothers persisted in working at their claims until well into the 1920s.

Meanwhile, it was Pioneer Canyon that seemed to draw the most attention and enthusiasm. The old claims were worked again and new mines were opened throughout the canyon. Lily M. Smith from New York obtained a series of claims about a mile out of town and opened the Dyke Tunnel, Silver Tip, New York Tunnel, and Rochester Tunnel. She built her cabin in the vicinity of the Hillside Tunnel near the point where the road first crosses Pioneer Creek. These Smith holdings were modestly successful and were worked off and on for over twenty years.

A half mile beyond the Smith claims lay the Moberg property. Soon after 1900 Harry Moberg acquired a group of claims which he would work for 25 years. Three different tunnels were opened and at the Midway Tunnel he built cabins and buildings. The Moberg family lived in these cabins at the mine site and remained here until Harry's death in 1935.

Further up the Pioneer Creek road and about three miles from town was the property of George (Lee) Crowe, an unusual character. Said to be a botanist and known as a world traveler, he appeared in Red River about 1920, acquired a mining claim and built a cabin on the property. He began developing a mine and eventually dug several tunnels extending 1,400 feet into the mountain. He is best remembered for the extensive rock garden which he constructed

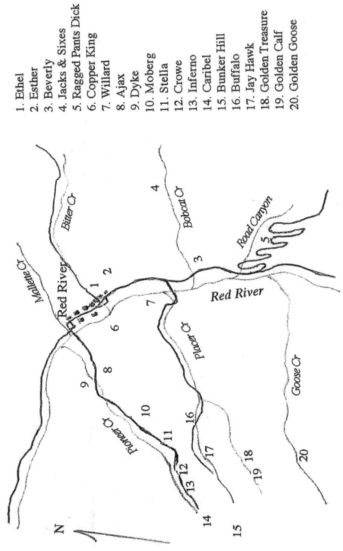

Red River Mining District

1. Ethel
2. Esther
3. Beverly
4. Jacks & Sixes
5. Ragged Pants Dick
6. Copper King
7. Willard
8. Ajax
9. Dyke
10. Moberg
11. Stella
12. Crowe
13. Inferno
14. Caribel
15. Bunker Hill
16. Buffalo
17. Jay Hawk
18. Golden Treasure
19. Golden Calf
20. Golden Goose

adjacent to the cabin. A portion of Pioneer Creek was diverted to form a waterfall and pond, and Crowe planted a variety of flowers throughout the property.(19)

At the end of Pioneer road and five miles from town was the Caribel mine, the most extensive and profitable operation of this period. In 1910, H.L. Pratt purchased claims from Andy Manson and Melville D. Pierce (the prospect was named for Pierce's wife, Caribel). Pratt organized the Caribel Milling and Mining Company and he was able to obtain financial backing through the A.H.A. Furu family of Trinidad, Colorado. Retaining Pierce as superintendent, Pratt expanded the site to include thirteen patented claims. An extensive building program resulted in the construction of cabins, bunkhouses, a cookhouse, an assay house, barns, and a blacksmith shop. Several hundred tons of ore was sent to the June Bug Mill and it produced eighteen dollars per ton. By 1917 there were 30-40 men working the mine and several families living in cabins on the site. A five-story building was constructed to

Lee Crow at his cabin and mine on Pioneer Creek
Picture courtesy of the Red River Historical Society

Buildings at the Caribel Mine in the 1960s
Picture courtesy of the Red River Historical Society

house additional equipment which included a 25 ton cyanide mill, stamp mill, a ball mill, and an ore crusher. The machinery was water powered by means of a ditch which brought water from Pioneer Creek. The Caribel remained profitable until World War I when the operation was curtailed due to the inability to raise additional capital. After the war the company was able to refinance and continued to function during the 1920s. (20)

The only truly significant, successful, and lasting mine in the Red River area was the Moly Mine located five miles west of town and

This view was taken inside the old Caribel mill and shows the large Separator Wheel, now located at the Red River Museum
Picture courtesy of the Red River Historical Society

halfway to Questa. Here, in about 1916 Ed Westoby and a partner discovered molybdenum ore. Samples were sent to Denver and other points for assaying but the message always came back, "pure graphite, with no value whatever." However, during World War I the Germans showed the world the value of armaments made of steel that had been hardened by adding molybdenum, thereby creating an important market for this ore. In 1918 Jimmy Fahey sent another sample for assay and this time the ore was recognized and its real value pointed out. Fahey then organized the claims as the R & S Molybdenum Corporation and sent several loads of ore to the June Bug Mill.

The following year the Molybdenum Corporation of America acquired the mine and began a huge building investment. By 1922 fifty miners were at work and within a few years the workforce had doubled. A large mill was installed, housing and cabins for the workers were built, and a large school was provided for the children of the workers (the Moly Mine School). The Moly Mine was soon recognized as one of the largest and richest molybdenum mines in

The Molybdenum (Moly) Mine
Picture courtesy of the Red River Historical Society

the world and by 1980 its total production had reached twenty million pounds (most of this coming between 1925 and 1945). During the Depression years the mine employed more than a few of the Red River citizens and it helped to boost the economy during the lean years.(21)

The mining revival, though somewhat short, helped the town of

The Molybdenum (Moly) Mine near Questa as it appeared in the 1920s
Picture courtesy of the Red River Historical Society

The Red River schoolhouse, July 4, 1925
Picture courtesy of the Red River Historical Society

The Moly Mine schoolhouse, used by Red River students for a number of years
Picture courtesy of the Red River Historical Society

Red River survive and provided a degree of economic stability for a time. While the surrounding gold towns of Twining, La Belle, Midnight, Anchor, and E-town were either empty or rapidly disappearing, Red River persisted, not necessarily thriving but more than simply hanging on. A continued flow of newcomers balanced out those that were moving on and, as some businesses closed, others seemed to take their place. In fact, during this period two new hotels were opened, the Penn and the Cole, and C.C. Clapper opened a general store.

In 1914 the schoolhouse burned, requiring a new building. The Red River School District, issued $3,000 in bonds to cover the cost and considered several designs. Apparently The Territorial Department of Education was consulted, for the finished structure closely resembled a model shown in *Designs and Specifications for New Mexico Public School Buildings*, a book produced by the Territorial department. With minor modifications the new building followed the "Design No. 2 for a One-Room Frame Building". The town hired a carpenter-builder, Ed Wheatcroft of Sunshine Village. Mr. Wheatcroft was said to also be a miner, rancher, and bootlegger but his talents as a builder were not questioned and he later became best known for his work on the new Red River Pass road. Using local volunteer labor, including the Mallette brothers and Ed Westoby, he completed the structure in time for it to open in the Fall of 1915. In that first year of operation the Red River Schoolhouse enrolled forty-five students in grades one through eight.

The schoolhouse served the community until around 1936 when the Moly Mine School came into being and Red River children were sent there for schooling. In addition, some of the teachers for that school were supplied by the town of Red River, most notably Winnie Hamilton, Dolly Johnson, and Nell Wagner. After 1958 the school children were bussed to the Questa schools and this continued until 1986. During the nearly fifty years in which there was no school in Red River, the schoolhouse was used for community meetings, some church services, and other gatherings. Through the years the school building had been painted white and in the 1960s the new Red River Women's Club painted it a bright red. It has been subsequently known as the Little Red School House and today houses a museum.

The mining industry, which had been slowly declining, was dealt a serious blow by the First World War which made both manpower and capital scarce. Industry created by the war effort drew many men away from the community and to other places. Investment money all but disappeared. When the war ended, efforts were made to put some of the mines back into operation but with limited success. By 1920 there were several mines working and these included the Caribel, Buffalo, Jay Hawk, Golden Treasure, Independence, and Orofino. These mines struggled through the subsequent ten years and all required infusions of money. Some of the miners, prospectors, and investors continued to hang on, reluctant to accept reality. Once again it was shown that gold fever, after taking a strong hold, is slow to cure. There were those who remained optimistic and continued to persevere in spite of obvious failures and disappointments. However, it would not be long before the Great Depression would arrive and effectively end any further hopes of gold mining in northern New Mexico.

TRANSITION
(1920 - 1950)

Shortly before 1920 there were two events, widely separated geographically, but which taken together would drastically alter the future of Red River. The first of these happenings occurred in the Red River Valley itself and was to a great extent brought about by efforts of the townspeople. After forming the Red River Good Roads Association, the citizens petitioned the National Forest Service to construct a new road which would replace the harrowing wagon road down the Big Hill through Road Canyon. This new route was built in 1915-16 and became known as the Red River Pass Road (today it is called the Old Pass Road). Although somewhat crude by today's standards, it was a remarkable improvement over the old road and gave much better access to E-town, Cimarron, Raton, and Springer. More importantly, the road was designed for automobile traffic, it became part of a state highway, and therefore put Red River on the map.

Meanwhile, more than 1500 miles to the east and hardly recognized by the people of northern New Mexico, another event was taking place in Dearborn, Michigan. Henry Ford was about to complete his River Rouge Plant which would soon be turning out Model T automobiles in great numbers and at a price affordable by the middle class. Soon America would take to the roads and the summer family vacation would become an institution.

These things happened at a fortuitous time, for the future of Red River appeared bleak. There were only a few mines still in operation and they were struggling. During World War I a number of people had left for better jobs elsewhere and only a handful had returned. The full-time population had dropped below one hundred fifty and continued to decline. This in turn meant fewer businesses and merchants. All in all, the very existence of the town seemed in doubt.

It was at this point that the townspeople began to notice a curious thing: there seemed to be an increasing number of summer visitors in the Valley. They were not interested in prospecting for gold and silver but instead came to simply enjoy the mountains with their beauty, cool summers, and clear running streams. Most of these strangers were from the plains of Texas, Oklahoma, and Kansas and they often came as families. Although usually staying only a week or two, they seemed to return year after year. Most importantly, they spread the word about the Valley and recommended it to friends and neighbors so that the number of visitors gradually increased.

The people of Red River soon realized that here was a new and different opportunity. It was time to turn to the other attributes of the Valley besides gold and silver, and to build a future on tourism and visitors. It was a time to provide lodging and meal service, to cater to square dancers, fishermen, hikers, and horseback riders. Some of the old-timers began to lead the way: The Oldham brothers came down off the mountain, built cabins and a lake, and opened Tall Pine Camp. Jesse Young quit his job in the Buffalo Mine, began building cabins on his homestead property, and developed Young's Ranch. The Brandenburgs remained in the meat and grocery business but opened a restaurant which would become famous for its "hot biscuits".

Slowly, gradually, the town began to grow once again and the economy to improve. This enticed a whole new group of people into the Valley, a different collection of entrepreneurs who would become permanent citizens and add their names to the list of "old-timers". They built lodges, cabins, restaurants, shops, stables, and stores, all aimed at the vacationers and visitors and by 1950 the list of these new establishments was impressive.

Some of the visitors began to buy or build summer homes and cabins. A number of these were located within the town itself, while others were along Bitter Creek, as well as south of town in the

Upper Valley. Although these "summer people" were not permanent residents, many would play an active role in the development and history of the town. In fact, one of the summer folks, Ruth Yeager, was the major force behind the building of the Community House which would become a popular institution in Red River.

Meanwhile, other things were happening. The National Forest Service worked steadily to improve roads, trails, and campgrounds in the Carson National Forest and this enticed more people to come to the area. The Fish & Game Department established a fish hatchery at Questa and from here stocked the surrounding lakes and streams, giving a boost to Red River's reputation as a mecca for fishermen. Telephone lines were strung up the canyon from Questa and it was not long before Rural Electrification reached the town. A modern water supply and sewage system soon followed.

By mid-century Red River had become a flourishing tourist community and even boasted of a Chamber of Commerce. It had become widely known throughout the Southwest and visitors came from a variety of states. However, the town was faced with a major problem. As a mountain tourist community, the business season was markedly short, three to four months at best. In September the visitors began to scatter and did not return till late May, creating a situation in which it was very difficult to make an adequate living because of only four months of business activity. As a result the population during the winter months dropped drastically, at times to less than a hundred people, so that most of the citizens were part-timers. What was needed was some kind of a year-round business climate.

At the urging of the townspeople of Red River, the Carson National Forest agreed to build a new road to lead over the pass and connect with Elizabethtown and Cimarron. In 1914 a surveying party came to the Valley to begin the task. The group was headed by Howard Waha, Forest Service Engineer, and among his helpers was a junior engineering student named Kenneth Balcomb. Two years later, in the final construction phase, Waha would go elsewhere and Balcomb would be in charge.(1)

This new road was to be designed for automotive travel so the surveyors were to meet certain criteria: the maximum grade on straightaways was to be seven and one-half percent; it would decrease to five percent for the one hundred feet approaching the switchback turns; the grade around the turns should be three percent; the radius of the switchback turns was to be not less than thirty-six feet; and a southern exposure was required to minimize winter snow problems. To meet all the gradient requirements a road of three and one-half miles was needed in order to allow for the thousand foot drop to the valley floor. The survey party decided there was one area that answered all the needs--a steep mountainside south of town and facing in a southwesterly direction. The new road would begin one-half mile from where the old road started down and would consist of seven long switchback legs, finally reaching the valley floor more than a mile south of town. The survey work began and by the end of that first summer it was completed.

The following summer, construction was started. The Forest Service team directed and supervised the work and hired most of the labor locally. The site itself presented several major problems, largely because of the steepness of the slope. Rocks, rubble, and dirt removed for the roadbed would often slide and tumble downhill, causing a minor landslide, thus endangering anyone on the slope below, and damaging any road work further down the hill. For this reason the construction was begun at the top of the mountain and progressed down the slope, a situation that was very inconvenient in the early building stages. The lower part of the mountain was more steep so as the road progressed downward the slides and rockfalls occurred more frequently and this became a real problem as the work neared the valley floor. It so happened that the property at the base of the mountain and below the new road consisted of a farm owned by Thomas Melson. He had homesteaded this site soon after 1900 and had built a cabin for himself and his wife, Mary. In addition to the house, there was also a barn, some sheds, and a fair sized corn field. Rock slides and boulders seemed to directly target the corn field so that by the end of summer very little corn remained standing. Surprisingly, Melson never complained, only expressing his gratitude that the road was being built.

Much of the work was done by hand using picks, shovels, crowbars, and dynamite. Large wing plows and beam plows pulled by a team of horses were used to loosen material and fresno scrapers, also pulled by horses, could move large amounts of dirt and rubble. Making the first cut with a plow was very difficult because the four abreast horses would be standing on the steep slope with the uphill two being much higher than the down-slope pair. This made it difficult to gain much traction and there was always the chance of one or more of the horses falling downhill. Part of this problem was solved by the chance hiring of a plow and fresno operator named Ed Wheatcroft. Wheatcroft owned a ranch at Sunshine Village, was well known as a jack-of-all-trades, and had been responsible for constructing the new school house. A colorful character, he provided his own team of very large horses. He directed and controlled this team by shouting in a loud voice while using an earthy and at times, rather obscene, vocabulary. The loud yelling, instead of frightening the horses, seemed to have a calming effect on them and Wheatcroft was always in absolute control of the team. He was given the task of making the first cuts of each of the switchback legs and he was able to do this more easily and quickly than anyone else.(2)

Work progressed and by summer's end much of the pass road was partially complete. The following year, 1916, the Forest Service team returned, this time under the direction of Balcomb who was now designated "Assistant Forest Ranger - engineer". A great deal of finish work remained and this included putting in culverts and drainage ditches. Much of this required hand work and a large crew was hired, mostly Taos Indians. Trees were generally cut off about three feet above ground in such a manner that they would fall uphill where they could be trimmed (any that fell downhill had a tendency to roll all the way to the bottom). The stumps were then dynamited. As construction neared the valley floor Tom Melson's house and property came increasingly in range of falling boulders and other missiles. On one occasion, Jesse Young, who was in charge of the dynamite crew, set too great a charge under a large stump. A giant chunk of wood hurtled through the air directly toward the Melson barn below. At the last minute it veered to one side, missing the barn but demolishing a large sled which was sitting beside it.

In spite of a few minor setbacks the construction proceeded at a smooth and steady pace so that by August the road was complete and vehicles began travelling down the mountain. The road itself had certain drawbacks: it was rough and unpaved, one-way in spots, and had fairly tight turns. It was situated on a relatively narrow ledge on the mountainside, had no guard rails or barriers, and was frightening for some people. Nevertheless, over a period of fifty years the Red River Pass Road came to be used by thousands of vehicles.

Soon after the road's completion, a trickle of autos began descending the pass and within a few years this had become a steady stream. The number of summer visitors gradually grew to several hundred; in ever-increasing numbers they came. In 1920, two of the Oldham brothers, Richard and Nathan, purchased the Melson property consisting of 31 acres lying just below the Red River Pass road. The Oldhams planned to use the Melson cabin for winter housing for the three mining brothers and also to begin developing accommodations for the summer visitors. In 1922 a small lake was built on the property and stocked with fish. Soon thereafter a few buildings were erected for the use of visiting fishermen. Thus began Tall Pine Camp, which would lay claim to being the oldest tourist camp in the Valley. Within ten years there were eighteen cabins, lots of visitors, and Tall Pine had become a successful business.

By the mid 1930s, the Oldhams, who were getting along in years, decided to turn the operation over to the younger generation. For the future management of Tall Pine they chose one of Nathan's daughters, Winifred, and her husband, Walter Hamilton. As things turned out, the choice could hardly have been better, for the Hamiltons would spend the rest of their lives in the Valley, become pillars of the community, and have much to do with the future success of Red River.

Laura Winifred Oldham was born in 1901 in Raton, one of four children of Nathan Oldham and Ada Stevens Oldham. Nathan, of course, had come west with his brothers, while Ada was born in

The old Red River Pass Road, completed in 1916. The body of water below the road is the fishing lake at Tall Pine Resort.
Picture courtesy of the Red River Historical Society

Elizabethtown, where her father owned a merchantile store. Later the Stevens moved to Raton and it was there that Nathan and Ada met and married. They had a total of four children: Winifred, two other daughters, Mabel and Florence, and one son, Nathan, Jr. who was known as "Red". Although Winnie would later declare that she had always wished to be an actress, the practical side of her nature led to a degree in Education from Highlands University in Las Vegas. Upon graduation and the return to Raton, her first teaching job was at Johnson's Mesa School. Later she moved to the school at Sugarite, the coal mining camp near Raton. It was here that she met Walter Hamilton and thus began a love affair that would endure over fifty years. They were wed in 1925 and for their honeymoon chose a camping trip to Red River, a fitting and auspicious omen of their future life together.

During the early 1930s, Walter and Winnie traveled to Nevada where Walter worked on the building of the Hoover Dam and Winnie continued her teaching. In 1935 they returned to New Mexico and became owners and operators of Tall Pine Camp. They began a program of renovating the cabins, adding new ones, and developing an office, meeting room, and a small store. They would later add a small restaurant. The name was subsequently changed to Tall Pine Resort and its operation became a family affair when Winnie's siblings, Mabel, Florence, and Red joined them in the management. Tall Pine came to be known as a family resort and many couples returned with their children year after year.(3)

At the same time, the Hamiltons gave much time and effort to the community of Red River. For several years Winnie taught the students at the Moly Mine School. In addition, she was a member of most of the organizations in town, several of them as a founding member (this included the Red River Woman's Club and the Red River Historical Society). Having a great interest in history, she authored two books dealing with the early days of Red River-- *Wagon Days in Red River* and *Reflections from Raton to Red*

TRANSITION

Tall Pine Camp located at the foot of the old Red River Pass
Picture courtesy of the Red River Historical Society

River, the latter written when she was ninety years old.(4) Winnie converted the old Melson cabin into a historical museum and filled it with artifacts and collectibles from the mining days. She would conduct tours through the museum and prided herself on describing and explaining the various items.

After Walter's death in 1977, Winnie continued to operate Tall Pine as well as take an active role in the community's affairs. She gradually became the matriarch of Red River and at the time of her death at age 97 she was recognized as its first citizen.

Not far from Tall Pine another tourist resort was being established by Jesse Young, the second son of B.J. and Lizzie Young. In 1907, a time when the future of Red River seemed bleak, B.J. Young returned to Colorado taking most of his family with him. Jesse, who had been born in 1884 and thus was 23 years old, decided to remain in New Mexico. Like others at that time he was forced to try his hand at a variety of different jobs and this included hauling freight, working in the Buffalo and Caribel Mines, helping in the construction of the Red River Pass road, at one time serving as Justice of the Peace, and even acting as a part-time dentist.

One of Jesse's accomplishments was his marriage to Augusta Mutz of Elizabethtown. A member of the well-known Mutz family of the Moreno Valley, she was the daughter of Hermann Mutz and sister to Emil Mutz. Jesse and Augusta homesteaded a piece of property just south of the town and along the Red River. During the 1920s when it became apparent that tourist accommodations were needed, they built a lake and a few cabins. Subsequently, more cabins were added, along with stables for horses, a grocery, gas pumps, and camping facilities. Thus was born Young's Ranch, which became a popular and well-known resort. In the early 1950s the Youngs added a restaurant to the list of amenities at the resort.(5) Like many of the other visitor accommodations, Young's Ranch became a Red River institution, drawing loyal visitors year after

Walter and Winifred Hamilton standing in front of the Tall Pine office

TRANSITION   123

Early picture of Young's Ranch, before 1950
Picture courtesy of the Red River Historical Society

year. A generation of young people grew up there and in later years would bring their own families back to the Ranch and to Red River.

Jesse and Augusta produced two children, Gene and Marie, who grew up in Red River. Gene would one day take over the operation of Young's Ranch and carry on the family tradition.

Within the town itself cabins were built and tourist camps established. Near the east end of the community C.C. Clapper constructed numerous cabins near his general store at High Street and Jayhawk and this enterprise became known as Grandview Camp. At the other end of town Three Canyon Camp was built at the mouth of Mallette Canyon (at the present site of the Eisenhut and Eidelweiss Condominiums). This was operated by the Cashions and by the late 1930s could boast of 18 cabins, a grocery, electric lights, and showers. Soon, other vacation accommodations would be built in various parts of town.

T.D. Neal, the founder of Eagle Nest, opened a merchantile store in Red River which carried supplies for fishermen, hunters, trappers and tourists. This was managed by Horace J. "Cap" Johnson. He and his wife, Mary, had come to Red River in 1923 following a thirty year period in which he had served as an Indian Agent in Oklahoma and New Mexico. He would later serve as the town's postmaster for a period of twelve years. In addition to the store, T.D. Neal Merchantile owned and operated several cabins along the East Fork of the Red River about seven miles south of town and near the Cannard cabin. These were used by fisherman, hunters, and vacationers.

Harry Brandenburg, who remained in the grocery business, purchased a building at the corner of Main and Mallette and converted it into a restaurant. His second wife, Lela, made the

Jesse N. and Augusta (Mutz) Young in front of the cabin built in the '20s, which was the kitchen of the old house.

Jessie and Augusta Young at Young's Ranch
Picture courtesy of the Red River Historical Society

eatery famous as "The Home of the Hot Biscuits" and it drew customers from throughout the county.(6)

Unfortunately, tragedy struck the second generation of Brandenburgs: Charles was killed in a mine explosion, Charlotte died in childbirth, and William drowned in a boating accident. Thus was left only John F. (Jack) to carry on the family tradition. As a young man he worked for a time in the Taos store established by his father and it was here that he met the young woman who would become his wife. Anna Loretta (Lottie) Hallinan was born in Ontario, Canada and became a school teacher. In 1910 she came to Taos to stay with her sister and here she met Jack Brandenburg. They were wed in 1912 and moved to Red River where they would live out their lives.

Like the other young men of those times, Jack worked a variety

Three Canyons Camp located in the west part of town near the mouth of Mallette Canyon
Picture courtesy of the Red River Historical Society

Pioneer Lodge in the foreground looking south along Pioneer Road toward the Playhouse in Pioneer Canyon
Picture courtesy of the Red River Historical Society

of different jobs. This included stints as a miner at the Caribel Mine as well as in the Pioneer mines owned by Lily Smith. At one time he went to Tercio, Colorado to work in the coal mines there (the same mines in which his brother Charles was killed). During World War I Jack worked for a while in California in the shipyards and on his return to Red River he again became employed by the Caribel Mine. He and Lottie had two children, Aileen and John, both of whom would contribute to the history of the town. Though still strongly attached to Red River, the Brandenburgs, like many others, would spend the harsh winters in a more agreeable climate, so during the 1920s the family wintered at Raton and here the children went to school. Subsequently, Lottie decided to apply for the position of Postmistress of Red River and in 1934 she was appointed to the job which she would hold for the next twenty years.(7) Henceforth, the family would remain in Red River year-round and the children would attend the local school. With Lottie busy in her new position,

TRANSITION

The Brandenburg store about 1950
Picture courtesy of the Red River Historical Society

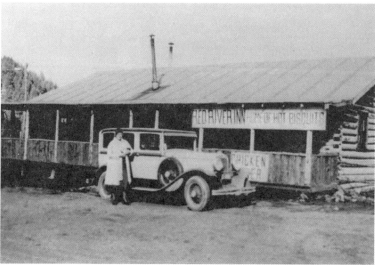

The Brandenburg building, "Home of the Hot Biscuits", at Mallette and Main. Today it houses the Red River Mining Company.
Picture courtesy of the Red River Historical Society

Jack decided to follow in the family's footsteps and opened a grocery and meat market.

The number of summer visitors continued to grow at a steady pace and this led to ever-increasing opportunities. More money and jobs became available and, as services for the tourists improved, this seemed to bring more visitors. Therefore, population and business activity in the community steadily spiralled upward. In the beginning, the bulk of the visitors came from the plains of Texas, Oklahoma, and Kansas, for from these areas it was a short distance to northern New Mexico and during the heat of July and August Red River's ideal summer climate beckoned. Visitors quickly learned that the Valley's prices were affordable and there were activities for all age groups. These characteristics made Red River an excellent vacation spot for families and the town's reputation began to spread far and wide. Those who came discovered a place of natural beauty, excellent climate, fine fishing, horseback riding, hiking, and camping. These were coupled with children's activities, square dancing, good food and church services. Altogether a combination that caused families to come back to the Valley year after year and to draw future generations to return with their own families.

They came from small towns and cities, ranches and farms, usually on the recommendation of a friend or neighbor. Many in turn would invite their own friends to join them in the mountains and in this way many communities sent large numbers of people, often out of proportion to their size. In 1945, the Red River *Colossal* reported that so far that summer, twenty-six families from Elk City, Oklahoma had vacationed in the community.

For some reason, a large number of visitors came from Wichita Falls, Texas and others were from Oklahoma City and the panhandle towns of Texas. As the word spread, visitors began to appear from farther and farther away. And still they came in ever-increasing numbers.

TRANSITION 129

One factor which has always enhanced Red River's attraction for visitors is that it is completely surrounded by National Forest. The pristine natural beauty has therefore been preserved, as has the wildlife, and through the years the Forest Service has done much to entice tourists. Beginning early in the 20th century, the concept of National Forests came into being and they were formed out of existing federally-owned property. In northern New Mexico, the Taos Forest Reserve and the Jemez Forest Reserve were partially combined in 1908 to form the Kit Carson National Reserve. Not long thereafter, the name was changed to Carson National Forest, the title it carries today. Bert Phillips of Taos became the first appointed ranger, serving until 1912.

During the first few years, much of the Forest was heavily logged, but this practice ceased completely in 1915. Not much later, because of the rapid increase in vacation travel, the Forest Service set as a

Summer visitors on horseback at the Pioneer Lodge in the 1930s
Picture courtesy of the Red River Historical Society

In Front of Red River Post Office & Hotel - 1934-35

(Not in order) Johnnie Phipps, Orin & Mrs. Ruggles, Bing Abbot, Marie Young, Mr. & Mrs. Pratt, Helen Cook, Bertha Pratt, Mr. & Mrs Penn, Mrs. Cook, Miss Reisenger (Teacher), Bertha & Ethel Pratt, Benn Miller, Tom Melson, Walter Janney, John Melson, Lyman Pratt, Cr. Clapper

Early Red River street scene in front of the hotel and post office
Picture courtesy of the Red River Historical Society

major priority the development of facilities and activities for tourists. As a result, a number of Forest Service roads were put in place, either by constructing new roads or improving the old network of mining roads dating back to the 1890s. In some places logging roads remained and these were cleared and improved. During the Depression, with the aid of the CCC, several campgrounds were built: Columbine, Bobita, Elephant Rock, and Junebug. Later the Forest Service began an ambitious program of developing a system of hiking trails throughout the high country and this work continued over a number of years. In the mid-1950s, jeep roads were built to both Middlefork Lake and Goose Lake.

For many years Truchas Peak, near Santa Fe, had been recognized as the tallest mountain in New Mexico. In the 1940s, a naturalist and mountain climber, H.D. Walter of Santa Fe, became interested in Wheeler Peak and suggested that it was actually the taller of the two. In July of 1948 he successfully climbed Wheeler from the Red River side and firmly established its height at 13,161 ft. In August of that year, the U.S. Geological Survey recognized Wheeler Peak as the highest point in New Mexico and this brought added fame and attraction to the Red River area.

Although the town was fast becoming a resort community, there were some who stubbornly continued to work the mines. During the 1930s the Caribel hung on, as did the Buffalo, and near the headwaters of Bitter Creek C.C. Lowe continued to work the Orofino. Not far away, the Edison Mine was reopened by new owners who contracted with Jack Brandenburg to see if new discoveries could be located. The most ambitious mining took place at the Black Copper, the site which in 1900 had seemed to carry the most promise of all the Red River mines. Around 1940, this mine came into the hands of Irene and O.B. Siler who were from Louisiana, where O.B. had been in the oil and gas business. The Black Copper was reopened, about twenty miners were hired, and the stamp mill was put back in operation, this time using a gasoline engine for power. When the ore had been crushed and washed, it was hauled to the smelter in Colorado Springs in dump trucks. For several years Siler was able to extract a modest amount of gold, but following his death the mine was closed.

One of the last of the old prospectors who still wandered the mountains, rechecking abandoned claims and looking for new ones was Joe Cannard. He had come to New Mexico in 1896 and found his way to Elizabethtown where he drove freight between Springer and E-town; later he was the stage driver to Red River. The lure of gold brought him to the Valley and here he remained. Cannard built his cabin in a lonely place nearly seven miles south of town on the East Fork and here he prospected and set out his claims. Joe

An early photo of Goose Lake

was somewhat odd and eccentric, renowned as a bear trapper and hunter; he claimed to have killed 48 bears in the area. He was also famous as a walker and hiker, at times walking from his cabin over the mountains to Taos and back. He frequently walked to Red River for supplies, a round trip of nearly fifteen miles.(8)

After T.D. Neal Merchantile built several cabins along the East Fork for vacationers, Cannard worked as a hunting and fishing guide. He was often regarded as a loner, almost a hermit. It, therefore, came as somewhat of a surprise to many of the Red River citizens to learn after his death that he was survived by a wife and two children.

Another old-time carry-over from the earliest days was Rebecca Coffelt who would gradually become known as the legendary "Aunt Becky". She was born in Trinidad, Colorado, a member of the prominent Moad family and was given the name of Rebecca Jane Moad. Her two brothers, Jarret and Granville, initially worked in the coal mines near Trinidad. On learning of the gold discoveries in

TRANSITION

Picture of Wheeler Peak taken in the mid-nineteen hundreds
Picture courtesy of the Red River Historical Society

northern New Mexico, they travelled westward, following the Purgatory River, reached La Belle and thence came to Red River via Anchor and Bitter Creek. They were among the earliest settlers in the Valley and built a cabin at the far eastern end of town near the Westoby cabin (High St. and Jayhawk today). They came to the valley each summer and early on introduced Rebecca and another sister, Cordelia, to the new community of Red River.

After Rebecca married Phillip B. Coffelt, a Santa Fe Railway engineer, she and her husband would frequently spend part of the summers in Red River. They built a cabin near the Moad and Westoby homes and this became the first dwelling place people would reach as they entered town from the east. Behind the school house and not far from the Coffelt cabin, the Moads staked out several mining claims and named them for Rebecca's children--the Esther, Stella, and Vesta.

Following Phillip's death Rebecca resided each summer in her cabin in Red River. She wintered in Trinidad and spent a great deal of time in travel, using her lifetime railroad "widow's pass". Through the years she became a well-known fixture in the town, and her home was always open to visitors, old and young alike. Anyone who stopped by her cabin was welcomed, especially children, and she became famous for her hospitality. Gradually, she became affectionately known as "Aunt Becky" and after a time, many knew her only by this name. She kept lists of her visitors, especially those whose travel led to the community from afar, and she would frequently send out cards to these people. Many would answer her, simply addressing their replies to "Aunt Becky, Red River, New Mexico".(9)

She became famous also for her flower plantings, which came to be known as Aunt Becky's Garden. This consisted of a large number of native wildflowers adjacent to her cabin which she would plant and tend lovingly.(10)

Aunt Becky died in 1945, having spent close to fifty years in Red River, and she was buried in Trinidad. Not long after, there appeared

The famous Joe Cannard holding one of his bear traps
Picture courtesy of the Red River Historical Society

Legendary "Aunt Becky" Coffelt at her house on High Street where she kept her large garden
Picture courtesy of the Red River Historical Society

in the Red River *Colossal* a flowery tribute to her written by Vernon Hendry. Among other things he said, "They laughed because Aunt Becky was fun, gifted with inimitable mimicry, her blue eyes dancing the while. Unconsciously perhaps, people themselves in harmony with the gay, clean, freshly-starched prints which adorned the ample frame of her tall figure; also with her gayer flower garden, widely publicized, where she might be standing alongside a giant blue delphinium as tall as she herself, with the columbine's prodigal bloom about her knees."

As the town of Red River gradually transformed itself into a resort community of some prosperity, a new group of citizens came to settle and make it their home. They opened a variety of new businesses, mixed with the townspeople, and contributed to the future welfare of the community. Many of them remained for a lifetime and to the next generations came to be considered as "old-timers". During the three decades between 1920 and 1950, the community received an influx of people who would in many ways be responsible for the future success of Red River. These "newcomers" included the names of: Mutz, Roemer, Wagner, Fink, Johnson, Lewis, Prunty, Booker, Zehna, Simion, Janney, Gwinn, Gallagher, and Patrick. After 1950 another wave of newcomers would appear and some of them would remain and take their place among the longtime citizens.

In 1925, following the death of his wife Julia, Orin Mallette decided to sell his property at the west end of the valley. At the time, this comprised about 110 acres (much of what is now the western part of the town of Red River), the buyer being Santiago Ortez of Questa, the price $4,500. Ortega successfully used the land to run sheep and this continued for four years until his death. In the settlement of the estate, the Red River property went to Jose Ortega, also of Questa and also a breeder of sheep. In 1936 the land was sold by Ortega to L.S. Lewis of Irran, Texas.

Leffy Sterling Lewis and his wife Jessie Alice had lived in Irran where L.S. supplied equipment for oil drilling. Both were involved in a major auto accident and following this decided to move to a cooler climate for the sake of their health. From friends in Wichita Falls they learned of Red River, came for a visit, and promptly moved to the area, bringing the three children: Evelyn, Clifton, and Lester. After purchasing the property, they moved into the Orin Mallette cabin and made this their home. L.S. soon built seven cabins for tourists and called the operation the Lewis Ranch. These initial cabins were rather rustic, and were supplied with a wooden cook stove, a water bucket and dipper, dishpan, and kerosene lamps. Maintenance and cleaning was done by Mrs. Lewis and the children. Horses were stabled at the ranch and made available to the visitors. Over the years other cabins were built, along with additional

TRANSITION

amenities and Lewis Ranch became a favorite destination for many visitors.

In 1936 Lewis began work on The Playhouse, a 6,000 square foot dance hall, located at the mouth of Pioneer Canyon (it still exists today and has long been operated by Bud and Betty Fisher). Although primarily a dance pavilion, The Playhouse also contained a bowling alley and later a gambling area. Gambling was actually illegal at the time but the laws were not strictly enforced so that gaming was carried on, especially in remote places like Red River. The Playhouse had slot machines, blackjack, roulette, and dice tables, all operated by Long John Dunne of Taos. At the time, there were two other gambling establishments in town, one run by Tony Simion and the other by Dan Zehna at the Silver Spruce Bar.

L.S. was engaged in several different enterprises, one of which

Early picture of The Playhouse built by L. S. Lewis in 1936. The horse pasture is today's location of the Alpine Lodge.
Picture courtesy of the Red River Historical Society

L. S. and Jessie Alice Lewis
Picture courtesy of the Red River Historical Society

was a saw mill. He had brought a tractor with him to Red River and he used this machine for a variety of purposes, including hauling logs for the mill.(11) In order to power the saw, he travelled to Dawson (southwest of Raton) and bought an old steam engine that had large solid iron wheels. He drove it to Red River, the entire trip requiring two weeks and ending with a daunting descent of the Red River Pass. At a later time, Lewis made a trip to Wichita Falls and purchased a large diesel engine to use as a electric generator. With this, he was able to supply electricity to The Playhouse and, in addition, sell surplus power to Pioneer Lodge and Three Canyons Camp.

The Lewis children grew up in Red River and Lester, who was the youngest, attended the Red River School and later the Moly Mine School.(12) During his tour at the Mine school, Winnie

Hamilton was his teacher. He described how his father sometimes had to plow the road to school using a grader propelled by the Lewis tractor. Later, Lester would play a prominent part in the community, running Lewis Ranch, The Playhouse, building the Powder Puff Ski Area, and opening a restaurant. He and his brother Clifton would also develop the Cliffside Cabins.

Among the many newcomers to the community were members of the Gallagher and Mutz families, who made the short migration from the Moreno Valley across the mountain ridge to Red River. John and Mary Gallagher had come to northern New Mexico in the 19th century and had settled on a ranch near present-day Eagle Nest. They produced ten children and two of them would play a role in the history of Red River. Maggie Gallagher married Emil Mutz, son of the well-known Herman Mutz of Elizabeth-town and they produced six children, one of whom, Johnny Mutz, made the move to Red River and made it his home. Another of the Gallaghers, Maurice, married Lula Phipps, who came from yet another prominent Moreno Valley family; she was the daughter of Albert W. and Ida Gilbert Phipps.

Maurice (Morris) and Lula Gallagher moved to the Red River area, first to the top of the Pass, and later to a cabin in Mallette Canyon. They had six children: Opal, Bud, John, Pearl, Maurice, and Herbert. In the 1930s, the Gallagher family opened a riding stable located at the mouth of Mallette Canyon, largely operated by Opal, Bud, and their father. At that time it was called the Gallagher's Riding Stables, but later, after Opal married Norman Guinn, the name was changed to Gallagher and Guinn Stable. In 1946 it was moved to High Street across from the School House. Subsequently, the stable moved to Main Street (present location of Patrick's) but then went back to High Street. Years later, Opal would lease land at Young's Trailer Park near Placer Creek and open a second stable. The Gallagher-Guinn stables would go on to become a landmark in Red River and, over a period of more than sixty years, would serve

Opal Gallagher Guinn with one of her horses
Picture courtesy of the Red River Historical Society

and delight thousands of vacationers.(13)

Bud Gallagher married Greta Goosman and the two of them, along with their children, spent summers in Red River on the Mallette Canyon property. Winters were spent in Raton where they owned a home and where Bud taught school, but come May the family would head for the high country where Bud assisted Opal in operating the stable. Later the Gallagher children (Tamara, K.C., and Michael) would also lend a hand and help with the horses.(14) A number of years later, Bud and Greta built a gift shop on Main Street which they named the Bobcat.

Johnny Mutz grew up in Elizabethtown, where his grandfather had been one of the early settlers and leading citizens. As a result, Johnny was well acquainted with the history and happenings in the town, as well as knowing many of the people. His boyhood was a time when the community was fast fading but still enjoyed some of its colorful background and townspeople. He attended school at E-town, Eagle Nest, and at Cimarron and then returned to work on the ranch in the Moreno Valley. Later he moved over the mountain ridge to Red River and it was here that he met a summer visitor, Henrietta Jones of Oklahoma City. They were wed in January of

TRANSITION

1945, made Red River their home, and have left a lasting mark upon the community.

Like some of the miners of the preceding generation, Mutz seems to have engaged in a wide variety of jobs, vocations, and types of work. He continued to operate his ranch in the Moreno Valley and also ran cattle in the Upper Red River Valley

Johnny Mutz
Picture courtesy of the Red River Historical Society

(including Goose Creek, Black Copper, and Fourth of July Canyons). For a number of years he served as a hunting guide and led horseback trips into the high country. Much of his life has been spent operating heavy earth-moving equipment and at one time or another he worked on most of the roads in the area. When the ski area was built, Johnny Mutz was involved in much of the construction. He and Henrietta (Hank to all those who know her) during one period purchased and operated the Aspen Park Guest Ranch and Johnny also operated a riding stable.

Over the years Hank and Johnny have been active in nearly all civic aspects of the town. Their three daughters, Jeannine, Jan, and June, now carry on much of the family tradition.

One of the most colorful couples to come to Red River was Tillie and Tony Simion who arrived in the 1930s. Tillie Welch grew up in Kansas, one of eight children raised by a single mother. Although

Tillie and Tony Simion standing on the steps of Tony's Bar
Picture courtesy of the Red River Historical Society

times were hard and all the children worked, Tillie was able to attend a state teacher's college in Pittsburg, Kansas and become a teacher. She met and fell in love with Tony Simion who worked in the coal mines in Girard, Kansas; they were married in 1922, and a year later a son was born, Tony, Jr. The Simions lived in Girard for the next several years, Tony working the mines and Tillie teaching school. When the Depression arrived, Tony was forced to look elsewhere for work. Leaving wife and child behind, he obtained a job in Dawson, New Mexico working in the local coal mines. The following year, 1930, he was offered a position at the Moly Mine, halfway between Red River and Questa and he accepted the job. Tony found a one-room cabin, sent for Tillie and Tony, Jr., and the family settled into rather rustic living conditions at the Mine. They remained there for four years and when Tony lost his job in 1934, the Simions moved to Red River.

After renting a cabin on High Street from the Horace Johnsons, Tony and Tillie opened the Evergreen Sandwich Shop (hamburgers, 15 cents; pie, 10 cents; coffee, 5 cents). Water was obtained from the river, there was no electricity and no indoor plumbing, but the shop was moderately successful. Then Tony acquired the first liquor license in Red River and the Simions were on their way. A bar and

TRANSITION 143

dancehall was built on Main Street next to the Sandwich shop and the entire establishment was named Tony's Bar and Tillie's Cafe. A water well was dug, an electric generator was installed and Tony was ready to take part in the gambling craze that arrived around 1940. For a short while he was able to corner the market on gaming and liquor, but soon he would have competition. Dan Zehna opened the Silver Spruce Tavern across the street (location of Bull-of-the-Woods today) and offered drinks, dancing, and gambling. Not far away on Pioneer road, L.S. Lewis provided gambling at The Playhouse.(15)

Tony, Jr. attended the Moly Mine School through the sixth grade. Then he, along with John Brandenburg and others, boarded at the home of Emil and Maggie Mutz in E-town so they might attend further school in Eagle Nest. Following this, Tony went to high school in Raton, this made possible by Tillie taking an apartment there during the winter months. After a stint at Amarillo Junior College, he entered the Service during World War II and afterward returned to Red River, where he married Betty Foster. Tony, Jr. and Betty would have two children, Tony and Tobette.

Tony's Bar and Tillie's Cafe on Main Street, in 1940
Picture courtesy of the Red River Historical Society

Tillie and Tony were quite active in the social and community life of the town and were leaders as well as joiners of various community organizations. Around 1950 they took over the Monte Vista Lodge and operated it for seven years. This lodge (at the corner of Main and Copper King) had been built in 1934 by John and Zoe Wagner, along with the Baucums, Helen and Judd. It was far ahead of its time and offered the nicest and most modern accommodations in town, providing indoor plumbing, electric lights from its own generator, and running water that was piped from the river. The Lodge had a coffee shop, excellent restaurant, and a small cocktail lounge. It was a great success and everyone wished to stay at the Monte Vista. Later the lodge would burn but fortunately for the Simions they had sold it before this happened.

Tony Simion died in 1952, apparently as a result of silicosis which he had acquired during his long years underground in the coal mines. Later, Tillie managed the Alpine lodge, while Tony, Jr. operated the bar and dance hall and Betty served as postmistress. In the 1960s Tillie entered into Republican Party politics in a serious way. She served as the party chairman for Taos County, was a delegate to two national conventions, and in 1972 held the position of presidential elector.(16)

Others continued to come to the town and open businesses. Ethel and C.H. Prunty arrived in New Mexico in 1919 accompanied by their son George and planned to settle in Sunshine Village. However, things did not work out and they subsequently moved to Red River, while Prunty worked at the Moly Mine. In 1921 a second son, Bob, was born (in Greeley, Colorado, where Mrs. Prunty went to stay with a sister during the latter part of her pregnancy). Ten years later Prunty purchased 13 lots at the corner of Main and Copper King; included on this land was the original Sylvester Mallette cabin. In 1953, six years after the death of Mr. Prunty, the family constructed a building which later became known as the Wigwam Trading Shop. Here the Pruntys sold groceries, antiques and tourist

The Monte Vista Lodge built in 1934, in its day the premier lodge in Red River
Picture courtesy of the Red River Historical Society

items. Subsequently, cabins were built on the property and were rented to visitors.

Bob Prunty worked in the Moly Mine for a time prior to World War II and then helped to manage the family business operation. In 1958 he became postmaster and he and his wife Esther ran the Post Office, which was then located alongside the Trading Shop in the Prunty building. Bob has been Red River's weatherman for a long time and his daily records go back for over fifty years.

Lyman Pratt (son of H.L. Pratt, operator of the Caribel Mine) built and managed the Rio Colorado but later sold it to the R.S Bookers. Mr. and Mrs. F.E. Munden opened the Riverside which was later bought by the Lotts. Near the western end of town, Will and Dolly Johnson built the Pioneer Lodge and added a store which sold groceries, fishing tackle, curios, postcards, and both hunting and fishing licenses. In addition, they provided a filling station, horses for rent, and a guide service. Dan Zehna owned the Silver Spruce Bar (present day Bull-of-the-Woods) and across from it he constructed The Lodge. John Wagner, the son of the original builders of the Monte Vista Lodge, together with his wife Nell built the El Sombrero, which later became the Sundance. Fae and Pat Patrick opened Patrick's Sport Shop and, not far away, Dr. Claude Chambers and his wife operated The Starr.

During the years before 1950, the bars, restaurants, and many of the townspeople had a need for ice and since there was no refrigeration machinery in the Valley, the only source consisted of the lakes and ponds frozen during the winter months. Accordingly, the annual ice harvest became a well-organized community affair. The favorite site was the lake at Tall Pine Resort and the customary time was around Christmas, for by then the ice had usually reached a depth of more than 15 inches. As the season approached, snow was regularly swept from a given area of the lake which had been chosen.

The ice was cut with ice saws which were about six feet in length and operated by hand. Tongs were then used to lift the ice blocks which were moved to the "ice house" located near the lake. Sawdust, used as insulation, was placed on the floor of the building and along the walls. After the ice had been stacked it was further covered with large amounts of sawdust and, if properly insulated in this manner, the ice would last until late summer.

Many people availed themselves of the lake ice and some built their own ice houses for convenient storage. Other lakes and ponds came into use including the ones at Young's Ranch. Elmer Janney was the first to employ a circular saw powered by a gasoline engine.(17)

One rainy night in 1939 a small group of summer folks met and began discussing the possibility of building some type of community

Picture of an early ice harvest at Tall Pine lake
Picture courtesy of the Red River Historical Society

meeting place for visitors. The five friends consisted of Ruth Yeager and Mrs. Walter Bachman of Wichita Falls, Texas, Vernon Hendry of Oklahoma City, and W.P. Foster and his daughter Wellene of Enid, Oklahoma. All were seasoned Red River visitors, some had acquired summer homes, and all had enjoyed the mountain community. At the time there were no expensive hotels or fancy restaurants, just mostly rustic tourist camps without indoor plumbing or electricity. Evening entertainment was provided by the bars, gambling rooms, and dance halls but there was no place suitable for children and families. There was an obvious need for some kind of community building to provide recreation for family members of all ages: games, singing, dancing, lectures, and religious meetings. The group decided to explore the possibility of such a facility and thus was born the Community House, a Red River landmark that is still present and which has been a source of enjoyment for several generations and thousands of people.

The first step was to find a location. It was discovered that when the original townsite had been platted (in 1895), a lot had been set aside and dedicated for a "Community Building or City Hall". This lot was still owned by Taos County, so a 25 year lease (at $1.00 per year) was worked out with the County Commissioners. Then serious work began. The original group was enlarged into an official committee, Ruth Yeager was elected leader, and a funding campaign was started. All types of devices were used to raise money including donations, raffles, food sales, and book reviews. The committee made appeals to all the merchants and $400 was collected, including one evening's proceeds from The Playhouse given by L.S. Lewis. By the end of summer, a total of seven hundred dollars was in the bank and it was decided to begin construction. The group arranged a contract with Walter Janney for the building of a 30 by 50 foot log cabin shell and this was completed over the winter. However, the building shell still lacked a roof, floor, windows, and doors.

The next summer saw a frenzy of building activity, nearly all done by volunteers. Walter Bachman, a summer visitor, was chosen as construction boss and a large number of people offered their time and efforts.(18) Soon a roof was completed along with the proper sub-flooring. Jack Munden of the Riverside Lodge put in the windows and Hal Yeager was able to obtain very fine doors from the Waggoner Building in Wichita Falls which was being renovated. Yeager also came up with some maple flooring from the old J.C. Penney store in Wichita Falls. Furnishings were donated by various people and, the following year, Elmer Janney built the fireplace.

The Community House Committee selected the first directors, Harry and Dia Trygg. Harry had previously worked as a coach and school principal and had just recently been released from the Service. That first summer the two directors arranged a very busy program of square dancing, game parties, children's activities, and

TRANSITION 149

bridge. Sundays were devoted to a morning non-denominational worship service and Sunday school along with a session of singing in the evening. This pattern of activities, set in the early years, is still followed today. Preaching is done by various volunteer pastors who might be visiting Red River and, in the beginning, the singing was led by Carl Miller.

Ruth Yeager continued to prod her committee to raise further money so that over time improvements continued to be put in place. Through a generous donation by Mr. and Mrs. Roy Dunning of Lawton, Oklahoma a Sunday school room was added. A kitchen was also built, lights and gas were provided, and Mrs. E.B. Madden of Wichita Falls donated a large number of dishes. Through a combined donation by Lyman Pratt, Tony Simion, and Dan Zehna, a piano was purchased. Through the years two more major additions were built along with a cottage for the directors.

From the day it opened, the Community House proved to be an immediate and huge success. For well over fifty years it has served the majority of visitors in one capacity or another and those who come to Red River look upon it as a special and vital part of the town. It stands as a monument to hard work, perseverance, town spirit, and cooperation between all those in the community.(19)

Conveniences and utilities were slow to come to the Red River Valley. The first telephone line was strung in 1925 by the Forest Service as part of an attempt to control any forest fires. Actually, two lines were put in, one to the top of Gold Hill and the other to Red River itself. The town phone was placed in the store of Cap and Mary Johnson on High Street where the post office was located. The Johnson store thus became the unofficial public telephone and message center and Mary Johnson would generally place the calls. The Johnsons later moved the phone service across the street to a slightly larger building. Here as many as six people might be seated comfortably while waiting to make their calls.

In 1936 L.S. Lewis tapped onto this line and others followed: the

The original Community House building, constructed in 1940
Picture courtesy of the Red River Historical Society

The Community House in 1976 after several additions
Picture courtesy of the Red River Historical Society

TRANSITION

Brandenburgs, Simions, Zehnas, Hamiltons, and W.A. Johnsons. Counting the Forest Service, this resulted in an eight-party line, which meant there were few secrets in the town of Red River.(20) In 1947-48, regular telephone service came to the community and soon there were over a hundred phones in the town. Also by 1947 the Rural Electrification had pushed electric power up the Canyon from Questa, allowing all in the town to have ample electricity. In the following decade regular water and sewage systems would be put in place.

During the decade prior to 1950 the third generation of those earliest founding settlers began to come into their own. Aileen and John H. Brandenburg grew up in Red River where their mother was postmistress and their father was in the grocery business. It so happened that when the Monte Vista Lodge was built in 1934 a young man from Chandler, named D.A. Campbell, was hired by the Wagners to do the wiring on the building. After the lodge was completed he decided to stay on in the town and not long after that he married Aileen Brandenburg. They settled into the community and subsequently built Deer Lodge which they operated for several years.

In 1941, John H. Brandenburg (known to his friends as "Johnny B.") had reached the age of twenty. In that same year a young lady by the name of Rosemary Frambers came to Red River to spend the summer working for the Brewers, who owned the Monte Vista at that time. The two young people fell in love with one another but their courtship was interrupted by World War II. John enlisted the following year and was sent to Europe where he wound up in a German POW camp. He did not reach home until 1945, but not long after, he and Rosie were wed, thereby beginning what would be a long and happy marriage.(21)

John and Rosie built the Siesta Lodge which they operated for seven years. Later he would enter the insurance business and open an agency in Taos. The two of them would then divide their time between Red River and Taos, although the former would always be their real home. The Brandenburgs had four children: Kathy, John David (J.D.), Helen Rosemary (Cokie), and Pamela Aileen (Pam).

Meanwhile, Gene Young met a young lady from Wichita Falls named Dorris Jones who came to Red River in the summers (her father, Sam Jones, worked for Dan Zehna at the Silver Spruce). Gene and Dorris were wed in 1943 and a year later a son, Harold, was born. The couple soon took over Young's Ranch and operated it for a number of years.

In January 1947, the Red River Chamber of Commerce was organized and John H. Wagner was elected the first President. Initial projects included an advertising campaign, sponsorship of the *Red River Rustler*, a newspaper for the tourists, and efforts to speed up the water and sewer system. The Chamber encouraged road improvements to Red River, especially Highway 64, and also made plans for an annual rodeo.

The December 1948 issue of the *Rustler* carried an advertisement of holiday greetings from the majority of businesses in town. The list is rather interesting:

Aspen Park Guest Ranch -
    Johnny and Hank Mutz
Black Mountain Play House -
    Mrs. C. O. Erwin and S. W. Stribling
Brandenburg Grocery -
    Mr. and Mrs. Jack Brandenburg
Buckhorn Cafe -
    Mrs. W. R. Loggie
Charlie's Machine Shop -
    Charlie and Marie Roemer
Community House

Conoco Service Station -
　George and Roque
Deer Lodge -
　D. A. and Aileen Campbell
El Sombrero Lodge -
　Nell and John Wagner
Fink Grocery and Market -
　Loyal and Luce Fink
Gamble's Grill -
　Roy and Grace Gamble
Gallagher and Guinn -
　Maurice, Johnny Buddy Gallagher
　Opal and Norman Guinn
Grandview Camp -
　Mrs. Paul Long and Rosemary
　Mrs Glenn Wallace and Jack
Hill's Cabins -
　Ray O'Neil
Mr. and Mrs. Elmer Janney
Mrs. Mary Johnson
Lewis' Ranch -
　Mr. and Mrs. L. S. Lewis
　Clifton and Maryjo Lewis
Monte Vista Lodge -
　Ed and Billie Rawls
Mountain View Cabins -
　Mr. and Mrs W.F. Sowders
Mutz Stables -
　Emil and Maggie Mutz
O. V. "Slim" McCombs
Navaho Lodge -
　Bob and Eclon McCaskill

Patrick's Sport Shop -
    Fae and Pat Patrick
Pioneer Lodge and Cabins -
    Mrs. W. A. Johnson
Prunty's Cabins -
    Mrs. C. H. Prunty and Bob
Red River Inn -
    Mr. and Mrs. Reed
Rio Colorado Lodge and Cottages -
    Mr. and Mrs. R. S. Booker and Bob
Riverside Lodge and Cabins -
    Kenneth and Beth Lott
Roemer's Cabins -
    Earl and Ada Roemer
Siesta Lodge -
    John and Rosemary Brandenburg
Silver Spruce Tavern -
    Dan and Opal Zehna
The Starr -
    Dr. and Mrs. Claude Chambers
    Mr. and Mrs. George Davis
Tall Pine Camp -
    Walter and Winnifred Hamilton
    Mabel Del Dossa, Nathan Oldham
Three Canyon Camp -
    Mr. and Mrs. Joe Faulhaber
Thunderbird Courts -
    Wade and Bertha Stribling
Tillie's Curio Shop -
    Mrs. Mae Bell Nicke
Tony's Bar and Tillie's Cafe -
    Tony and Tillie Simion
    Tony, Jr. and Betty Simion

TRANSITION 155

Twin's Cafe -
 Cleta Bell Black and Leta Nell Tucker
Wagonwheel Courts -
 Mr. and Mrs. Bob Jones
Young's Dude Ranch -
 Mr. and Mrs. Jessie Young

YEAR ROUND RESORT
(1950 - 1970)

In the years following World War II great change swept over the entire country. Marriages postponed because of the war years now took place, the baby boom soon followed, and the increasing number of young families moved to the suburbs. A growing economy and plentiful jobs along with general prosperity led many of these families to find themselves in the rather enviable position of having more disposable income at the same time as increased leisure time. This led to a growing interest in new and different leisure-time activities and these included the wintertime sports of downhill and cross country skiing as well as snowmobiling, winter camping, and sledding. Downhill skiing, especially, seemed to grab the fancy of Americans and as a result there was a rapid move to construct ski areas and resorts throughout the Rockies. Fortunately, the town of Red River was able to be a part of this movement and to develop its own ski area. This changed everything.

By 1950 Red River had become a well-known and successful resort catering to several thousand visitors each summer. However, the fact that visitors were limited to the three or four summer months each year meant that the town would never have much future. There simply was not enough business activity in this short time to sustain any kind of permanent population. In fact during the early 1950s it was not unusual for the winter population to drop to less than forty individuals. Most of the summer townspeople closed their establishments and left the area until the following May. What was needed was some kind of strong business during the winter so that the citizens might work year round. The Red River Ski Area made this possible and within less than ten years the permanent (over winter) population would be close to three hundred.

The presence of a ski area in Red River was the inspiration of an Oklahoman named Stokes Bolton who came to the Valley in the 1950s. A man of vision, hard work, and ingenuity, he quickly realized what a ski resort could do for the future of the town and promptly set out to make it a reality. As construction got underway, Bolton had the foresight to hire as manager, Buzz Bainbridge, who had been in charge of the Santa Fe Ski Area. In a similar move, Bainbridge then traveled to Aspen, Colorado and hired Toni Woerndle to operate the Ski Area. The leadership group thus assembled proved to be highly effective so that when the ski area opened in the winter of 1959-60 it became a great success.

Now the summer resort of Red River had become a year-round community and this created rapid change as well as many new opportunities. The town began to grow and the winter population rose to several hundred. New housing appeared (especially condominiums) along with a variety of new business establishments. The highway was paved through the middle of town creating a new Main Street and this began to rapidly fill with new buildings. The highway to Questa was improved and soon there would be a new and modern road down Bobcat Pass, replacing the Old Pass Road. These moves transformed the highway access into Red River making travel quick and easy for the growing number of summer and winter visitors. At the same time a paved highway was extended south of town six miles into the Upper Valley and this opened the way for development of homes in Valley of the Pines, Monte Vista, and in the East Fork Canyon.

With all the new activity it was inevitable that a new group of people would be drawn to Red River to open new businesses and become part of the exciting growth. Many of these people would remain in the town, and within twenty-five years would become a new generation of old timers. Among the names were Calhoun, Williams, Woerndle, Frye, Bowser, Buchanan, Miller, Grindstaff, Tweed, and Lamb.

By 1975 the town was ready to make the final leap into being a modern community of the Twentieth Century.

In 1953 Stokes Bolton and his wife Audrey (known to many as Billie) began coming to Red River as summer visitors having been introduced to the area by a friend. Their home was in Oklahoma City where they owned and operated a hardware store and paint manufacturing company. It was not long before they had purchased land in the town and built the SEB Motel, located at Pioneer and Main streets (it became the Alpine Lodge). The experience as a local businessman brought home to Bolton the problems faced by the town merchants in trying to make a decent return in the short business span of only three to four months. A year round resort was needed and one way to accomplish this was with a ski area.

Bolton originally approached three other persons in the community about such a venture: John Brandenburg, Garnett Frye, and Lester Lewis. A partnership was considered and some of the group traveled to Colorado to examine different ski resorts. As things turned out, Bolton decided to pursue the idea on his own and a partnership never materialized. In December of 1957 Stokes and Audrey signed a use permit with the Carson National Forest for eighty acres to be utilized by the "Red River Ski Resort".(1) Workers were hired locally who began the tasks of clearing parts of the forest for various ski runs as well as bulldozing roads and other trails (some of this work was carried out by Johnny Mutz). For much of the steel supplies and pipe, Bolton scoured the Oklahoma oil fields for surplus equipment. In doing so he discovered some oil derricks which he was able to modify and use for the chair lift towers. By the middle of 1959 the majority of the construction had been completed. A double chair lift 5800 feet long was in place along with a 900 foot rope tow on the beginner's slope, and

Construction of the Red River Ski Area, 1958.
Picture courtesy of the Red River Historical Society

the runs, trails, and roads were about finished. It was time to make plans for the overall operation.

Bolton needed an experienced manager and fortunately he was able to hire A. W. (Buzz) Bainbridge, who was managing the Santa Fe Ski Area at the time. Bainbridge had been with the Santa Fe resort for four years and his wife, Jean, was a member of the Ski School there. Both of them were agreeable to moving to Red River and becoming a part of the new resort. They arrived during the summer and Buzz proved very helpful during the final period of construction.

Bainbridge began a search for someone to manage the Ski School. He traveled to Aspen, Colorado and there persuaded Toni Woerndle to come to Red River. Toni made a trip to New Mexico in December of 1959 and assisted in the opening of the ski season that winter. In February Toni purchased the SEB Motel from Bolton and then moved his wife, Ilse, and their two sons to Red River. Both Toni and Ilse were originally from Germany, having met while climbing in the Alps. At the time Toni was working as a mountain guide and ski instructor in Garmisch Partenkirchen while Ilse was employed in the family publishing business in Stuttgart. Eight months

YEAR ROUND RESORT 161

The early Red River Ski Area. The main lift house is to the left.
Picture courtesy of the Red River Historical Society

after that first meeting they were married and spent the next two years in Garmisch Partenkirchen before immigrating to the United States. The couple traveled to Colorado where Toni found employment at the Aspen Ski School. Ilse worked several different jobs until the Woerndles were able to purchase an old villa which they converted into an inn. It was given the name of Alpine Lodge and operated in the European style, providing lodging and two meals a day. It was in Aspen that their two sons, George and Rudi, were born. Toni subsequently moved to the Stein Erickson Ski School at Aspen Highlands and it was from there that he was lured away by Buzz Bainbridge and convinced to move to northern New Mexico.

The SEB Motel was renamed the Alpine Lodge by the Woerndles in keeping with their previous inn in Aspen. Toni developed and ran the Ski School while the lodge was largely Ilse's responsibility. She had not planned to cook any meals since the lodge restaurant had already been leased out to Harold and Tinkie Maroney. Unfortunately, it was not long before it became necessary for the Maroneys to return to Texas so Ilse was forced to step in and once again be in charge of a kitchen. With time and hard work the Woerndles were able to make the Alpine a success. Over the years several major additions and renovations were carried out to give the place a more alpine appearance; trees and flowers were planted and the grounds were landscaped. The Alpine gradually became the attractive establishment it is today.

The Woerndle boys were raised in Red River and later attended high school in Colorado Springs. Rudi became a lawyer, married Sandra Simpson, and joined a law firm in Midland, Texas. George remained in Red River where he built and operated the Sitzmark, and in 1997 he married Carol Madewell. George has been very active in civic affairs and has served on the town council.

A 1958 view of the Bolton's SEB Motel
Picture courtesy of the Red River Historical Society

After Toni Woerndle's death in 1981 at the age of 66, Ilse continued to operate the Alpine Lodge. She finally sold it in 1991 to Jerry and Verna Henson, leaving her time to spend with friends, children, and grandchildren.

The Ski Area opened in the winter of 1959-60 and the occasion was marred by the burning of the Monte Vista Lodge. This lodge had been built in 1937 by John and Zoe Wagner and was considered by many to provide the most desirable visitor accommodations in the town. It provided running water, indoor plumbing, electricity throughout and possessed an outstanding restaurant and bar. The Monte Vista ownership had passed through several hands, including the Tony Simions. On New Years Eve a fire broke out in the attic and went unobserved for a period of time, enabling it to grow to considerable size before it was detected. Attempts by the Fire Department to control the blaze were not successful, due in large part to the weather. The temperature was very low (some reports of 40 degrees below zero) and as water was pumped from the river it would freeze in the metal nozzles. As a result the Monte Vista was a total loss but fortunately no one was injured.

Ilse and Toni Woerndle in the 1960s
Picture courtesy of the Red River Historical Society

Looking down the chair lift toward the main lift house, 1960. The road running from lower left to upper right is Pioneer Road which ends at High Street. Notice that there is no Main Street extending eastward beyond Pioneer.
Picture courtesy of the Red River Historical Society

That first ski season drew only a small number of visitors and many business establishments remained closed through the winter as was customary. However, gradually the number of skiers increased and more lodges and restaurants found it profitable to be open for the winter visitors. As a result, the town slowly became a more year round resort. Before 1960 the wintertime population of Red River usually dropped to less than fifty people. Within a short time the over-winter (and therefore the permanent) population had grown considerably, reaching several hundred. A building spurt ensued, not only housing for the townspeople but also for the growing number of visitors. This included condominiums such as the Eisenhut and Edelweiss.

Bolton was responsible for several other innovations. With a group of partners he organized the Pioneer Water Consumers Association, a co-op to supply water to the town. A pond was built in

Pioneer Canyon near the location of the Dyke Tunnel and pipe was laid to parts of the western end of town. Eventually about fifty homes and buildings were included in the system. Bolton also built a movie theater in the SEB building (later the Alpine Lodge) and was responsible for bringing television to the town.

In 1962 the Boltons decided to sell the Red River Ski Area and it was purchased by a group of investors called Mt. Wheeler Development Co. The major stockholder and director of the group was Dr. J. B. Veale of Pampa, Texas. A couple of years later the Boltons left Red River and returned to Oklahoma City, led in part by the failing health of members of their family. Stokes died in 1987 at the age of 84 and Audrey died not long after. Their two children, Paul and Jean, still reside in Oklahoma City.(2).

Stokes and Billie Bolton standing beside their airplane
Picture courtesy of the Red River Historical Society

The Powder Puff, a beginner's ski area located in the west end of the valley
Picture courtesy of the Red River Historical Society

Not long after the Red River Ski Area opened Lester Lewis built a beginner's ski slope at the west end of town near the Lewis Ranch. This was named the Powder Puff and quickly became a favorite of first time skiers. It featured short runs of gradually increasing difficulty, a short tow rope, and a short chair lift (novices could learn the art of getting on and off the chair lift without embarrassing themselves). Snowmaking equipment was used to insure that the area was always supplied with powder. Many a flat lander first learned about skiing at the Powder Puff and it was very popular with visitors. In 1971 Lewis sold this beginner's ski area to John and Judy Miller along with Gary and Fran Starbuck. The Millers were relative newcomers to Red River but would spend most of their lives in the town, would devote themselves to the community, and would later join the list of old timers.

John Miller had grown up in west Texas but was really no stranger to Red River since his family owned a cabin in the Upper Valley and he had spent summers here for many years. He traveled to the University of Colorado to study geology and it was there that he met Judy Dorrance who was living in Denver. They became engaged and were married the day following their graduation. After a stint in the Navy and several years spent in Amarillo they moved to Red River in 1963. John initially worked at the Red River Ski Area and there became friends with Gary Starbuck who was the ski school director. John was employed at the Moly Mine for several years but after the two couples purchased the Powder Puff, the Millers devoted most of their time to that business. All of the partners helped in the instruction of novice skiers, Judy served as loud speaker announcer, and John and Gary maintained the equipment. (3) It was during this time that John began offering lessons in cross-country skiing and for this activity groups were taken to the Upper Valley which at the time contained only a few houses. From this early beginning the Millers later developed an extensive cross-country ski operation at the top of Bobcat Pass known as the Enchanted Forest.

John and Judy Miller have always taken part in civic and community affairs and the list of their contributions is extensive. Both have been active in the schools and the Chamber of Commerce, while John served two terms as mayor and Judy currently sits on the Governor's New Mexico Trails Committee. In 1976 John established the the Enchanted Circle Bicycle Tour which is still held on an annual basis.

The four Miller offspring grew up in Red River. John, Jr. is now a professor of physics at the University of Houston, and he and his wife, Karen reside there. Mary now lives in the state of Washington with her husband, Bill Tyers while Linda and her husband, Dave Mieras, reside on Mackinac Island. Ellen, the only child to remain in Red River, married Geoff Goins and is now the news editor for the Sangre de Christo Chronicle. In spite of raising a large brood, operating several businesses, and being very busy in civic affairs, the Millers continue to find time for the great outdoors, often spending whatever spare time is available in hiking and exploring the high country.(4)

In the 1960s the New Mexico Highway Department began the redesign and construction of several highways in and near Red River and this transformed the ease and convenience of getting to and from the town. In 1962 it was decided to straighten and pave Highway 38 within the town limits and this produced the present day Main Street which extends through town in a straight line. Prior to that time there was a large marshy area lying east of Pioneer Road and there were no streets in the area. The highway coming in from Questa detoured around this bog by turning north at Mallette Road one block and then running east along present day High Street. At about the location of today's Town Hall it angled toward the south, followed present Main Street until it crossed

Main Street before it was paved. The building on the left is the Riverside Lodge
Picture courtesy of the Red River Historical Society

Bitter Creek, then once again turned north a block to High Street which it followed out of town. The Highway Department filled part of the marsh and raised the level for the road several feet. This made it possible for the highway (Main Street) to follow its present straight line course.

This construction had the added effect of of opening up the central part of town for development since now filling in the rest of the marsh would make available the property between Main Street and the River. Much of this area was owned by Dolly Johnson, widow of Will Johnson and owner of the Pioneer Lodge. She sold one section to Stokes Bolton who in turn sold it to the Calhouns for the construction of Der Markt. Another section was bought by Johnny Mutz who sold it to Barney Chapman as the site for construction of Lifts West. Between these two pieces of property was a lot which became the location of a service station later operated by Roy Brunson. East of Lifts West was a large piece of property owned by John Brandenburg which later became Brandenburg Park.

A couple of years later the Highway Department returned to the area, this time to build a new pass road. The Red River Pass Road (called the Old Pass Road today) had been completed in 1916 and was approaching fifty years of age. It was antiquated and not in keeping with more modern standards. The road was unpaved, rocky, and quite narrow in spots. In fact, in a good many places it was not wide enough for cars to pass so that one would have to stop and back up to a wider passing area. In addition the road was perched on the side of a steep mountainside and there were no guardrails or barriers of any kind. Traversing the Red River Pass Road was daunting at best and downright frightening to many. Snow or ice compounded the difficulty. It is still surprising that during its time this road brought thousands and thousands of vehicles into Red River.(5)

The Highway Department decided to bring the new road down

View of the Upper Valley showing the large number of summer homes. Picture made in 1996.
Picture from the J. R. Pierce collection

through one of the canyons leading from the ridge to the Valley floor, thus avoiding the long switchbacks used previously. Newer and more modern equipment made it possible to use such a direct route. As to which canyon to use, there were two choices - Fourth-of-July Canyon or Bobcat Canyon. After discussion and deliberation it was decided to use Bobcat Canyon. This produced the Highway 38 route over Bobcat Pass that we have today which is located about one mile north of the old road. This new highway was not only quick and easy but also very safe and well maintained in winter.

Not long thereafter another road was built, this time a paved highway from Red River extending six miles south into the Upper Valley. Prior to that time there was a rough and unpaved road which traversed parts of the Upper Valley and several homes had been built in this area. In 1935, Francis Miller, Carl Miller, and Paul Armstrong purchased 128 acres in the Upper Valley, which was divided into lots of varying sizes. The development was dubbed "Querinda" (meaning desirable) and over the years the lots were sold and a number of summer cabins were built. Various of the Miller family built cabins along with the Dulaneys, Lathams, Freeses and Smiths. Most of these cabins were not accessible in winter and their use was limited. With the arrival of a paved road into the area much of this changed and more of the homes came to be winterized and put to use during the winter ski season.

The Upper Valley highway opened much more of the land for development. Valley of the Pines was surveyed, electricity was brought in and lots were sold. Success here led to further developments in Monte Vista, Wheeler Village, and Hidden Valley. Within the next thirty years several hundred homes would come to dot the area.

All of the changes in and around Red River resulted in an influx of newcomers and many of these people would remain for years, leaving their distinct mark upon the community. In the early 1950s Garnett and Thurline Frye came from Oklahoma and opened their first store, Frye's Western Wear and Sports Shop. Half a century later there would still be a Red River business carrying the Frye name.

Thurline, daughter of George and Lovilla Trego, grew up in Woodward, Oklahoma. As a young girl she became active in rodeo competition but often found it difficult to find proper western clothing. As a result her parents established the Trego Westernwear Manufacturing Company during the 1930s and it became a thriving business. Thurline later married Garnett Frye and their own daughter was given the name of Lovilla. The Fryes became a part of the manufacturing operation and in 1950 came to New Mexico, fell in love with Red River, and decided to open the Western Wear and Sports Shop. Later they opened a second store, the Arrowhead, located on Mallette Street.

In 1958, Lovilla Frye married Gary Bowser, her high school sweetheart, and the young couple began visiting Red River each summer to assist in the family business. By chance, it was in 1962 that Gary and Lovilla were put in charge of the Arrowhead. This also happened to be the year in which the Highway Department built the new Main Street and this resulted in much of the traffic along Mallette drying up, eliminating most of the Bowser's business. It was clear that to become successful the store should be located on the new Main Street so Frye decided to move. He arranged for Elmer Janney to build a new store on Main and this he called Frye's Country Store which soon became Frye's Old Town. It grew into a

Gary and Lovilla Bowser at the Arrowhead store, 1962
Picture courtesy of the Red River Historical Society

Red River institution and is busy today after nearly forty years.

Not long after the new store opened, Garnett conceived of the idea of special entertainment for the summer visitors in the form of a Wild West Melodrama, built around a shoot-out between bank robbers and the local sheriff. Frye wrote the script while family members and employees served as actors. The main action was preceded by a series of Indian dances performed by a group from the Taos Pueblo. This show, held outdoors at Frye's Old Town, was such a huge success that it came to be shown three days each week and is still enacted today. Over the years it has been witnessed by thousands of visitors and has become an integral part of the Red River scene.(6)

For many years Frye's Old Town was only kept open during the summer months while the Bowsers and Fryes would return to Oklahoma each fall to oversee the other family business. When Garnett retired and decided to remain in Woodward, Gary and Lovilla took over the management of the Red River store. The Bowsers produced two children, Tyler and Toni. Tyler's wife, April, proved to be a natural for the Old Town business and was placed in charge of the operation (one result of this is the fact that under her management, the store is now open year round). The Bowser's daughter, Toni, married Ed James and now resides in Enid, Oklahoma.

In 1960 Glen and Bernice Calhoun and their two children, Ted and Glenda came to the Valley. At the time they were living in Ft. Worth where Glen was employed by Safeway. The Calhouns had been urged to visit Red River by a friend, Tom Head, who owned Deer Lodge and who later developed the Edelweiss Condominiums. The Texans were struck by the beauty of the area and Glen decided to open a grocery, Glen's Superette, located at High Street and Bitter Creek, this in spite of the fact there were two other groceries in town, Fink's and Johnny Brandenburg's. For the first couple of years the store was open in the summer season only, the

Two views of Frye's Old Town in its early days
Picture courtesy of the Red River Historical Society

Frye's Old Town as seen in 1997
Picture courtesy of the J. R. Pierce collection

Calhouns returning to Ft. Worth each winter. As the ski season became more popular and the town began to grow, Glen and Bernice decided to make Red River their year-round home.

Because of the continuing rather short visitor season the Calhouns found it necessary to expand into other forms of business so they opened a gift shop and Glen began preparation to obtain a real estate license. Fortunately, his opening of a realty office came at about the same time that the Upper Valley highway was built, leading to development and home building in that area. Calhoun was chosen as the primary agent for the Valley of the Pines addition by John Hay, the general manager and was similarly picked by J. B. Veale, developer of Monte Vista. Glen Calhoun Real Estate quickly became a major success.

When Ted Calhoun completed his college work at TCU he made the decision to return to Red River and enter the grocery business. The Calhouns purchased the Brandenburg store on Main Street, renamed it the Red River Grocery and for the next five years it was operated by Ted and his wife, Beth. By 1970 Ted was anxious to build a larger and improved store so the Calhouns obtained property on Main Street that was owned by Stokes Bolton. A large building was constructed which housed Der Markt, the grocery, and also served as a location for the real estate office. Glen's Superette was closed along with the Red River Grocery allowing Ted and Beth Calhoun to manage Der Markt while Glen devoted his time to the realty operation. This arrangement also allowed Glen to devote more time to various civic activities which included serving as president of the Chamber of Commerce for four years.

In 1975 the Glen Calhouns retired from their Red River ventures and returned to Ft. Worth (and later to Weatherford, Texas). Ted and Beth remained in Red River and raised their three sons: Matthew, Ryan and Michael. Both of the Calhouns became very active in community affairs, Beth in the Women's Club and Community House, Ted serving as Mayor.

One of Red River's landmarks had its inception when Frances and Dexter Walthall moved from Lubbock, Texas in 1955. From a friend, Richard Matheny, they purchased property and two cabins located on High Street at Bitter Creek. After obtaining a jeep tour franchise they opened Dexter's Jeep Tours along with Dexter's Trading Post in one of the buildings. The Walthall's business operations proved to be successful and they enjoyed their life in Red River. In 1964 tragedy struck with Dexter's sudden and untimely death. Frances opted to continue living in the town and she was determined to keep up management of the trading post. Four years later she married Don Williams, a salesman out of Denver, and not long after the store was enlarged and renamed Williams Trading Post, the title it carries today.

Through the years Williams Trading Post became a favorite of summer visitors, young and old alike. In addition to the usual gift merchandise, it carried extensive fishing supplies since this was

Der Markt building in 1997
Picture courtesy of the J. R. Pierce collection

YEAR ROUND RESORT 177

Dexter's Trading Post on High Street in 1960
Picture courtesy of the Red River Historical Society

an area of Don's enthusiasm and expertise. Over time the store has remained popular and successful, many loyal customers returning year after year.

Frances Williams became one of a handful of people responsible for much of the preservation of Red River's history. She was a founding member of the Red River Historical Society and a board member for a number of years.. Along with others, she set about collecting artifacts, memorabilia, papers, various documents, and photographs, and then helped to promote a museum in which to house these items. In addition to her contributions to the Historical Society, Frances spent many hours as a worker for the Community House and the Red River Library.(7)

Another Red River landmark, the Riverside Lodge, was purchased by Terry and Letha Allen in 1961. Construction on the Riverside was first begun by Jack Munden back in 1928 when the town was still under the spell of gold seekers. Munden had operated the lodge for twenty years before selling it to Kenneth and Beth Lott who owned it twelve years before selling to the Allens.

Terry Allen had first discovered Red River as early as 1956 when he came to the area on a camping trip with several of his friends. When he and Letha married three years later they spent their honeymoon at Red River so it was only natural and fitting that they would return and purchase the Riverside. During their early years the Allens opened the lodge only during the summer tourist season, returning to San Marcos, Texas during the winter months so that their two daughters, Cindy and Becky, might receive their schooling there.

In 1973 the Riverside was modernized and winterized and in the following years it remained open year round. At one time the lodge housed a restaurant that was capable of seating eighty people. Through the years the Allens have continued to enlarge and improve the Riverside until it became what it is today. In later years Cindy Allen married Craig Swaggerty and they both would help in the management of the Lodge. (8)

In the fall of 1962 a group of women serving on the election board gathered to help supervise the voting; they were Winnie Hamilton, Dorris Young, Tillie Simeon, and Lottie Brandenburg. It is said that during the day's conversation, Winnie made the suggestion that they form a club which would combine social and civic activities. The idea was met with enthusiasm and the Red River Women's Club was born. Tillie was elected president, Winnie as secretary-treasurer, and 64 members were signed up (this must have included most of the women in the town).(9)

The Club's first project was to improve the town cemetery. A fence was placed around the old portion of the cemetery along the west side. Here are located graves of some of the early settlers including the Mallettes and Westobys and some of the burial sites are either unmarked or display only some random stones. A bronze plaque was placed upon a stone marker to denote the significance of the site.

YEAR ROUND RESORT

Frances Williams on horseback in the 1960s
Picture courtesy of the Red River Historical Society

Another early project of the Women's Club was the repair and upkeep of the School House. This building had been built in 1915 and used as the Red River School, but beginning in 1941 the school was closed, with the children being sent to the Moly Mine school and later to Questa. The building was subsequently used as a town meeting place for a number of years until the Women's Club took it over. A twenty-five year lease on the building was first obtained from Taos County (how the county received title is not clear). At the time the school was white in color but the women decided to color it a bright red, using paint provided by Stokes Bolton. Ever thereafter it has been known as the Little Red School House. After gas heat was installed and new wiring was put in place, the building was furnished with tables and chairs. It became a meeting place for the Club but was also used for a variety of town meetings.(10)

The Women's Club in its first year established the Annual Christ-

Texas Red's Steakhouse on Main Street, 1996
Picture courtesy of the J. R. Pierce collection

mas Dinner which is still held after forty years. There is also the Halloween Carnival held annually to entertain the children while also serving as a fund raiser. Through the years money raised by the club has been used for a variety of projects and these include a Scholarship Fund for Red River high school graduates and the purchase of children's playground equipment at Brandenburg Park.

The Red River Ski Area continued to grow in popularity providing employment for the townspeople (11) and also bringing ever increasing numbers of visitors each winter. This in turn led to more opportunities for newcomers. In 1967 Bill Gill and his wife Annette came from Texas where he had been an oil lease broker. That first summer he operated an arcade but in the fall he and his brother John and sister Martha Gill Stephens decided to open a restaurant. John's Jeep Trailways building was remodeled and by Thanksgiving they opened with the "Great Steakburger" as the main menu item. However, it quickly became apparent that much more money could be made in serving quality steaks so the restaurant became a steakhouse. At about this time John Gill was an actor in Frye's Melodrama where he played the outlaw, "Texas Red". The name seemed to stick and was soon transferred to the Gills' restaurant, and thus Texas Red's Steakhouse was born. It was a huge success so two years later a downstairs lounge was added and in 1975 major additions were added to the dining area as well as the lounge.

Texas Red's became well known for its excellent steaks, unusual menu, the custom of dropping peanut shells onto the floor, and its reputation has grown through the years. The restaurant has remained a family affair with most of the members working in some capacity at one time or another. One son, Rick, remained in Red River while the other son, Ralph, moved to Dallas (and naturally worked in a steak house there). Janetta, the daughter, remained in Red River and is a real estate agent.(12)

Verlyn (Bud) and Betty Fisher arrived in Red River in 1958 and their names came to be associated with another landmark, the Playhouse. It had been built in 1936 by L. S. Lewis as a dance hall but it also contained a bowling alley and in the early days had served as a gambling establishment. E.B. and Nona Madden had bought it and later it came to be owned by the Madden daughter, Billie and her husband E.D. (PeeWee) Martin. It so happened that the Martins placed an advertisement for a couple to come and operate the Playhouse during the summer months and Bud Fisher answered the ad.

Both of the Fishers were born in small towns in Kansas and had met at McPherson College. Bud became a high school teacher of Industrial Arts and also served as a coach. At the time most teachers were paid on a nine months basis so they would generally seek some kind of employment in the summer. In 1957 Fisher answered the ad offering a summer job in Red River so he and Betty along with children Sandra and Randy came to the Valley. The Playhouse still served as a dance hall but the bowling alley had become a major attraction and there were also games and an outdoor miniature golf course. The pin boys were from Questa and lived in in small cabins adjoining the Playhouse. Bud and Betty were forced to work long hours, seven days a week.

After two years the Fishers decided not to return to New Mexico but in the summer of 1960, PeeWee Martin suffered a heart attack and found it necessary to move to a much lower elevation. The Playhouse was up for sale and the Fishers took advantage. For the next twenty years they would spend their summers in Red River and return to Kansas for the winter so that Bud could carry on his teaching. Their third child, Barry, was born in Red River and at various times all of the children helped in the operation of the business. Oftentimes Bud was able to convince some of his students to spend their summers in New Mexico where they worked for the Fishers. When the last child had finished school, Betty and Bud were able to move to Red River full time. On occasion they would be able to find someone to manage the Playhouse allowing them to devote time to other endeavors. They came to operate the Go-Karts on Main Street in addition to building several rental apartment units. And like most very busy people the Fishers have given much time to the community, Bud through the Chamber of Commerce, and Betty serving in the Women's Club, the Historical Society, and the Friends of the Library.

The Buchanans, Don and Loveta, came to town in 1970. Although Don had visited Red River as a child he had not returned to the area. After their marriage the Buchanans lived in Albuquerque a short time and then in Denver for nine years. Don had always wanted to return to the New Mexico mountains so they decided to make the leap, giving up their jobs, selling their home and travelling to Red River in a trailer. Don went to work with the Highway Department which was building the Upper Valley Highway and Loveta found employment as a secretary at the Moly Mine.

The year after arriving the Buchanans purchased the larger por-

The Starr building on Main Street, owned by the Buchanans, in 1997
Picture courtesy of the J. R. Pierce collection

tion of the Starr building and opened a gift shop. Later they were able to obtain the remainder of the building which had housed a small barbecue business. For a while Don continued to operate the barbecue shop but later closed it and consolidated everything into a single operation. In addition to its gifts the Starr became well known for its extensive line of fly fishing equipment as well as an outstanding inventory of fine knives.

The Buchanan's daughter, Heather, was born in 1972. She attended school in Red River, Eagle Nest, and also the Taos Christian school. Don and Loveta were insistent that she attend Sandia Prep in Albuquerque so each winter Loveta and Heather would temporarily leave Red River and spend the major part of the school year in Albuquerque, leaving Don to operate the store. After finishing college Heather married Bill Fredrickson and they moved to Albuquerque.

During this period others came to town and opened various busi-

Russel's Pond on the East Fork, built by T. A. and Madge Russel
Picture courtesy of the J. R. Pierce collection

nesses: T. A. and Madge Russell who built a home on the East Fork opened Russel's Gift Shop.(13) Robert Coss bought El Western while Ray and Lottie Tweed operated the Highlander Restaurant. Roy Brunson retired from his position as sheriff in Claude, Texas, came to Red River and purchased the service station between Der Markt and Lifts West. The Pendleys built the Friendly Pendley's Motel on the Westoby property (it later became the Lazy Bear Lodge). Woody Taylor opened the Casual Shop while Clinton Woody built the Village Inn. Pat and Mary Lamb operated All Seasons and the Patrick Shop was begun by M. O. and Faye Patrick (it was later run by their daughter, Maxine, and her husband, Bill Grindstaff).(14)

Meanwhile, members of the old families continued to contribute to the community. Lester Lewis, in addition to operating the Lewis Ranch, built the Powder Puff and also opened the Big Chief Trading Post (in the building where Capo's is now located). Later he turned the trading post into the Homestead Steakhouse but it only lasted three years. Lester and Jan's son, Brett, later managed his own steakhouse (Bretts Homestead Steakhouse) in the Lewis home on the River Ranch property. Lester's brother Cliff, in cooperation with their father, L. S. Lewis, had built cabins at the west end of town across the highway from the Lewis Ranch. These were named Cliffside Cabins and were operated by Cliff and his wife Mary Joe for a number of years. Cliff worked as an engineer for Phillips Petroleum and the couple lived with their three children in Borger, Texas. In the summer months, Mary Joe and the children came to Red River to manage the cabins and Cliff would arrive on the weekends.

At the other end of town both Tall Pine Resort and Young's Ranch continued to remain popular with the summer visitors. The Hamiltons, Walter and Winnie, along with Winnie's siblings Mabel,

The Big Chief, a trading post, built by Lester Lewis. It now houses Capo's restaurant.
Picture courtesy of the Red River Historical Society

Gene and Dorris Young with their son Harold in 1961
Picture courtesy of the Red River Historical Society

Florence, and Red, continued their labor of love to maintain the success of Tall Pine. Next door at Young's Ranch Jesse and Augusta Young, the founders of the business, had produced two children, Marie and Gene. In 1943 Gene married Dorris Jones, a summer visitor from Wichita Falls and it was not very long until the young couple took over the operation of the ranch. They in turn would eventually relinquish the management of Young's Ranch to their son, Harold.

John Brandenburg and Rosemary (Rosie) Frambers were married in 1945 and built the Siesta Lodge which they managed for seven years and following this the couple owned and operated a grocery store on Main Street. In the mid-sixties John decided to enter the insurance business and opened an agency in Taos which meant they would subsequently divide their time between Taos and Red River though the latter remained home to them. The Brandenburg children were four in number: Kathleen (Kathy), John David (J.D.), Helen (Cokie), and Pamela (Pam). Kathy married

YEAR ROUND RESORT   187

Mike Vukonich and lives in Raton, Cokie and her husband Rod Dickinson reside in Clovis, while Pam is wedded to Cecil Kite and they live in Eagle Nest. J.D. and his wife Renay remained in Red River where they manage the Red River Mining Co. and the Lonesome Pine Pub. J.D. also spends time in the insurance agency in Taos. Renay and J.D. produced a fifth generation of Brandenburgs, Kori, Jessica, and Justin, all of whom grew up in the community and added their own contributions.

Bob Prunty became postmaster in 1958 and served in that capacity for almost twenty-seven years. He and his wife Esther opened the post office in the Prunty building located at Main and Copper King.(15) In addition to his work with the mail, Bob continued his long habit of keeping regular and detailed records of the town's weather.

John and Rosie Brandenburg and their family
Picture courtesy of the Red River Historical Society

INCORPORATION
1970 - 2000

As the last quarter of the twentieth century approached, the town of Red River had become a successful and well known resort community. During the summer months several thousands of visitors came to the Valley to enjoy the the mountain climate, natural beauty, trout fishing, hiking, camping, and jeep touring. In winter thousands more would come to participate in downhill and cross country skiing, sledding, ice skating, and riding snowmobiles into the high country. The Chamber of Commerce was hard at work promoting special activities in the late spring and early fall in an effort to extend the tourist season and make the community a more attractive place in which to live. By now the permanent population had reached about three hundred and many condominiums and summer homes continued to be built. All of this seemed to point to a rather promising future. However there was lacking one important ingredient--the town still did not have any central governing body or focused direction.

This changed in 1971 when the town of Red River became incorporated and this move opened the door to a number of new opportunities. Now the township was eligible for more state money, it could levy taxes, and could issue development bonds. The town's newly elected officials turned to planning for much-needed infrastructure such as water, sewage, lighting, and street improvements. This would be followed by the building of parks, a library, museum, and a municipal building. A variety of new opportunities had suddenly become possible and many of these were acted upon.

The Red River Ski Area was becoming more popular and drawing an increasing number of winter visitors. In 1975 it was enlarged and improved by adding new lifts as well as new runs. Several years later John and Judy Miller opened the Enchanted Forest, a cross country ski area located near the top of Bobcat Pass and it would not be long before this became one of the premier cross country facilities in the state. As a result of these and other factors the winter revenues soon exceeded the summer time numbers.

As the population continued to grow, so did the need for new housing and as a result a number of homes, condos, lodges and cabins were built in the western end of town until the land was gradually filled as far as the River Ranch. The eastern part of the community also grew and enlarged until it reached the old Young's Ranch property. Here Harold Young developed a portion of the acreage into homesite lots which were quickly sold and developed. Beyond the town limits an ever increasing number of summer homes went up. Cabins and homes were built in Bitter Creek canyon, some of them on land leased from the Forest Service. The Upper Valley contained a large amount of private property which was rapidly turned into lots for homesites. Valley of the Pines, Monte Vista, Querinda, Wheeler Village, Hidden Valley, and the East Fork area all seemed to sprout homes and cabins so that by century's end there were about as many homes and dwellings outside the town limits as there were within the town itself.

In March of 1971 the citizens of Red River voted by a two to one margin to incorporate and then selected their town leaders: David Stults as Mayor; Councilmen Lester Lewis, John Miller, Ted Calhoun, and P. W. Lamb; Municipal Judge D.G. Dabbs; Town Clerk Martha Stephens. Rules and procedures were drawn up and the town embarked upon several tasks. The most pressing need was a municipal water system to replace the Pioneer Water Consumers Assn. and the collection of random wells then in use. The following year plans were drawn and the town council requested money from the state. A grant for $420,000 was soon forthcoming and construction got underway in 1973. A 1.25 million gallon reservoir was built in Pioneer canyon along with a treatment facility and an extensive piping system was put in place. The new water system proved to be a vast improvement and now the townspeople could be assured of a plentiful supply of pure water.

Of next importance was the need to upgrade, repair and enlarge the rather crude sewer system then in existence. Much of this had been built in 1971 and operated through a Users Association. The town purchased the system in 1974 and took over its management. There was much need for repairs and upgrading because of extensive leakage throughout the system. This consisted not of leaks out of the collection of pipes but rather leakage of underground water into the system so that much more water was reaching the treatment plant than had been expected. In fact the amount of flow through the pipes was five times what it should have been and was beyond the capacity of the treatment facility. Outside consultants were brought in and a long range plan was established to gradually control all of the leaks.

In 1974 Red River embarked on the development of its first park and chose a site in Mallette Canyon. After gaining approval from the Forest Service (because of the park's location), the town obtained funding of $42,000 from the New Mexico Bureau of Outdoor Recreation. This provided enough money to carry out initial development and build tennis courts and a basketball court. Two shelters, playground equipment, tables, and benches were added and the park opened in 1975. Twelve years later the town planned a second park, this time in the very heart of town on Main Street. A large piece of land was purchased from John Brandenburg, extending from Main to the River and lying east of Lifts West. Here the town of Red River gradually built various amenities and began a long program of landscaping. Eventually a large Conference Center would be constructed here.

192   INCORPORATION

Another order of business was the need for some type of building to house the town's offices, meeting rooms, employees and records. In late 1976 a large grant was received from the Economic Development Administration and plans for a 12,000 square foot structure were drawn by an architectural firm in Albuquerque. This building would house the town administrative offices, the town marshall, and provide space for the volunteer fire department. When the Town Council met to consider approval of the plan, a great furor broke out over the architectural design, a number of townspeople feeling the structural design was not in keeping with the western frontier and alpine flavor of the majority of Red River's buildings. The meeting went on for hours and many spoke in opposition to the plan until it appeared the new building would be voted down. As things turned out, it was too late to change the design since the grant stipulated that construction must begin within ninety days of the awarding of the money or else it could

Construction of the Red River Town Hall, 1977. In the background is Frye's Old Town.
Picture courtesy of the Red River Historical Society

INCORPORATION

Looking down the Red River Ski Area toward the town--in the 1980s
Picture from the J. R. Pierce Collection

not be used. By now, the deadline was only three weeks away and there was no time to redo the plans, so a contract was promptly let to begin construction. The building was completed, became the Town Hall, and with time came to be accepted by the citizens.(1)

The number of winter visitors continued to grow as the Red River Ski Area became better known and more popular. By 1976 the proceeds to the Town from winter tourists began to surpass the summer proceeds. About this time the ski area owners drew up a long range plan designed to provide facilities to handle triple the number of skiers. A number of years would pass and there would be a change of ownership before all these plans would be put in place but eventually the ski area would be transformed into what it is today. On additional land obtained from the Forest Service the number of ski runs and trails would be gradually increased to a total of nearly 60, some now extending on the south or back side of the mountain. New chair lifts would be built including a major one in the middle of town and the facilities at both the base and the top of the mountain would be enlarged and improved.

In the early 1980s the Mt. Wheeler Development Co. and its major stock holder, J. B. Veale, decided to sell the ski area. A real estate firm in Amarillo was hired to manage the sale and two realtors, Chuck Hix and George Blanchard began making arrangements. Both George and Chuck were well acquainted with Red River, Chuck having spent time as manager of Mountain Shadows. After some consideration they decided to form a group and offer to purchase the ski area themselves. The duo organized a corporation, the Red River Ski Area, with George Blanchard as president and Drew Judycki serving as vice-president and general manager.(2) The other stockholders were Chuck Hix, John Evans, and Sam Colson. An offer was made to Veale for the ski area and the sale was completed in 1984.

About this same time John and Judy Miller opened an area for Nordic or cross country skiing located at Bobcat Pass. John had become interested in teaching cross country skiing during the time he and Judy were co-owners of the Powder Puff. During those years he would take groups into the Upper Valley which at the time contained almost no buildings, just large open meadows. After the Millers sold the Powder Puff, they opened a shop in the Lifts West building but later moved across Main Street and the store became known as Miller's Crossing. In 1985 John was able to obtain from the Forest Service a lease on over 1,000 acres near the top of Bobcat Pass. To this he added 270 acres of leased private land and thus was able to put together nearly 1,400 beautiful acres which the Miller's named the Enchanted Forest. Nordic ski trails were cleared, groomed, and ultimately extended a total of 28 kilometers. Facilities also included a warming hut, benches, tables, and shelters. By 1992 the Enchanted Forest was recognized as northern New Mexico's largest cross country ski area and that season the Millers recorded over 8,000 skier-days. Geoff Goins

INCORPORATION

John Miller cross country skiing at the Enchanted Forest
Picture courtesy of the Red River Historical Society

manages the Enchanted Forest and the Millers are able to provide skis, clothing, and equipment for Nordic skiing through their store, Miller's Crossing.

The Red River Library began in 1982 when Fanny Bliss, then age 80, retired and moved to town to be near her daughter, Evelyn Clarke. Fanny had lived in Clovis, New Mexico and had played a prominent role in the Curry County Library located there. Soon after arriving in Red River she set about promoting a local library and began raising money. At her suggestion the town council and Mayor John Miller organized a library board and appointed Fanny Bliss as its first president.(3) Before the year was out the board had raised over $4,000 and had collected 2,500 volumes donated by locals and some of the summer visitors. A small but usable amount of space in the council chambers was set aside and the Red River Library was open for business.

The Red River Library--photograph made in 1997
Picture from the J. R. Pierce Collection

By the end of the next year the town council had voted a small operating budget and it was not long before the Friends of the Library came into being with Lee Romig as president. This organization set out to raise $10,000 and meanwhile provided volunteer librarians such as Tinkie Maroney and Kay Magruder. In 1989 the town council selected Romig to be official librarian She had had previous library experience and by the following year had catalogued over 4,000 volumes under the Dewey Decimal System. The Friends of the Library continued to offer financial support and this allowed the library to consistently grow and serve more people.

By the early 1990s the library had outgrown its space and there was a growing awareness that larger quarters were needed. A petition was presented to the town council requesting the consideration of a library-museum complex to be constructed in Brandenburg Park. This idea was initially met with considerable favor and plans were drawn for such a building. However, opposi-

INCORPORATION 197

tion arose over the location since some insisted that the Park should not be disturbed but remain a green space in the center of town. The plans were put on hold but all was settled in 1993 when the Bull Pen restaurant building at the east end of town became available. It was purchased from Roland and Mary Ann Betz and also some surrounding property was bought from Johnny Mutz. The building was soon renovated for a library and one large room was set aside for a museum. At about that same time Lee Romig resigned and the town council subsequently selected Kerry Shepherd as the new librarian. Kerry who had come to Red River with Fritz Davis four years earlier was experienced in teaching, library activities, and computer work. With an improved budget from the town council she increased the number of books, continued the job of cataloguing, and added computer resources to the library.

With the consistent help from Friends of the Library in terms of money and volunteer assistance, and under Kerry's direction the library continued to grow in size and complexity. By the end of the century, although the building had been expanded and the museum had moved next door, the library still seemed short on space. At this time it now contained over 13,000 volumes, a number of which were children's books. In addition to a large number of books of fiction, the library held audio books, videos, CD's, reference works, a Southwest Section, a variety of magazines, and five computers for public use, some with Internet access.(4)

The Red River Historical Society was born in 1984 when a group of interested people came together to form an organization for the preservation of the history of the area. A constitution and by-laws were drawn and the first officers elected: Harold Young, president; Francis Williams, vice-president; Judy Brunson, secretary; Joe Janney, treasurer. There were also seven directors.(5) By the end of the year there were a total of 33 members and at the close of the century the membership had grown to over a hundred.

The Historical Society has presented numerous meetings and

programs emphasizing the town's colorful history in an attempt to educate the citizens about their past. From the beginning a major effort of the group has also been the gradual collection of a variety of historical material: artifacts, photographs, books, notes, letters, obituaries, newspaper articles,etc. These were accumulated and held in hopes that someday a museum might be built. In 1993 when the library opened in its new building a room was designated as the museum and the first displays were arranged. Lee Romig began the task of organizing and cataloging the collection of written material.

Fritz Davis and Kerry Shepherd, having first come to Red River in 1989,began publishing the Red River Miner in 1993 with Fritz as Editor and Kerry as Publisher. This newspaper was purposely modeled after the early town papers and its major thrust has been to educate its readers about the colorful historical background of Red River. Several special editions were produced, each devoted to some aspect of the town's background. Alyce Densow wrote a number of articles about many of the pioneer families and individuals, most based on interviews and reviews of oral history which she carried out.(6) A number of stories were written about the town's early citizens and merchants, the early mining days, and various events of the early decades. All of this helped to elevate the level of historical interest while giving a boost to the historical society. In the 1990s the Little Red School House became available and was purchased from the Questa School District. A fund raising effort was headed up by the historical society and money was raised to refurbish and move the building to its present location where it was designated as the Red River Museum. A portion of the building was arranged to resemble its original use as a school house with desks, maps, blackboard, some of the original books, and a teacher's desk. The remainder of the museum houses the large collection of artifacts and photographs. Once the new museum became a reality the pace of historical acquisitions acceler-

The Red River Museum, housed now in the Little Red School House. The flowers are in memory of Aunt Becky's garden.
Picture from the J. R. Pierce Collection

ated as more families and individuals came to realize the importance of the museum as a repository for Red River's history.(7)

The town's population continued to slowly increase as new people came to the community and made it their home. John and Linda Hoag were originally from Virginia and like many others came to the area almost by accident. After graduation from college in 1972, John set out on a tour of the country and by happenstance landed in Red River. He worked here for a short time , then returned to Virginia where he and Linda were married. The young couple came to northern New Mexico, settled in Red River, and have never left.

The Hoags purchased the El Sombrero which at the time contained thirteen cabins and nine rooms. They soon put in a Mexican food restaurant, named it the Sundance, and as it became more popular began to slowly reduce the number of rental accommoda-

The Red River Inn as it is today
Picture from the J. R. Pierce Collection

tions. The dining room was later enlarged and a gift shop added so that eventually their interests were centered in the Sundance restaurant. By the end of the century it it had become a Red River landmark.

Alyce and Ken Densow first came to the area in 1975 as visitors. At the time they were living in Wisconsin where Ken was a school administrator and Alyce worked as a journalist, serving as an editor and columnist. They were so taken with northern New Mexico that they returned the following year, purchased the Red River Inn, and became permanent members of the town.

After several years the restaurant at the Inn was closed and replaced with a gift shop (later there would be several gift shops). Ken also built a theater which became known as the Mine Shaft Theater and here were shown a wide variety of shows and forms of entertainment. The most well known entertainer to perform at the theater was Michael Martin Murphy who developed a special

INCORPORATION

relationship with the Densows and as a result, he has appeared at the Mine Shaft on numerous occasions over the years.

Ken served on the town council while Alyce became known for her historical articles which appeared in the Red River Miner. In these she interviewed a number of the town's citizens and by means of their memoirs and oral history Alyce was able to examine and develop a better picture of Red River's history. The Densow's children, Linda, Kathi, and Jerry, became a part of the Red River Inn and together with their spouses made the operation a family affair.

Ann and Mel Tompkins along with their three daughters, Susan, Laura, and Karen, came from Little Rock in 1977 and purchased the Red River Merchantile. However, during the winter of the following year the store burned and was a total loss. The Tompkins moved to Santa Fe but three years later they returned to Red River and purchased the Patrick shop. This store had been managed for

The Red River Town Hall--1998
Picture from the J. R. Pierce Collection

years by Bill and Maxine Grindstaff and before that by Maxine's parents, the M. O. Patricks. Mel worked as a sales representative and the entire family helped out in Patrick's.

In 1995 Mel died after a lengthy illness and although the girls had married and moved away Ann elected to remain in Red River. She still operates the Patrick Shop and has become a long time member of the community.

As the last decade of the twentieth century approached several of the old time families still remained in town. There were three generations of Brandenburgs: Rosie and John continued to split their time between Taos and Red River; J. D. and Renay operated the Red River Mining Company and the Lonesome Pine Pub; The youngest generation of Kori, Jessica, and Justin attended school and worked in various of the establishments. Lester and Jan Lewis remained in the community and Brett Lewis opened Brett's Homestead Steakhouse located on the old Lewis Ranch property. Harold Young owned and operated a sanitation company but sold it and then built a campground and R-V park at the east end of town which proved to be very popular and successful. Later he and Angela decided to develop the old Young Ranch property for private homesites.

Winnie Hamilton, who had managed Tall Pine Resort after the death of her husband, Walter, came to be recognized as Red River's first citizen. She died at age ninety-seven and it was noted that her life span had closely approximated that of the town. She had first come to the Valley at age sixteen to visit her uncles and she and Walter had later made Red River their home. Winnie celebrated Red River's centennial when she herself was ninety-four.(8)

Other of the oldtimers remained, either active in business or community affairs. These included Gary and Lovilla Bowser (Frye's Old Town), Betty and Bud Fisher (Playhouse), Letha and Terry Allen (Riverside), Loveta and Don Buchanan (the Starr), Mary and Pat Lamb (All Seasons), Frances and Don Williams (Williams

INCORPORATION

Trading Post). Annette and Bill Gill were at Texas Red's, Linda and Ted Calhoun at Der Markt, and Henrietta and Johnny Mutz took part in various town activities. Judy Brunson became the Town Clerk while Johnny operated Calhoun Real Estate. Although the Tweeds retired, Lottie devoted many hours toward landscaping and beautifying the town while Bob Prunty continued to faithfully keep records of the weather and served as museum guide.

The town of Red River continued to grow and develop so that by the end of the century the population was approaching five hundred (in addition, there were close to six hundred summer homes and cabins scattered about outside the town limits). Jake Pierce became Town Administrator in 1988 and under his guidance the local government continued to improve the infrastructure of the community, especially the water and sewage systems. In the early 1990s the New Mexico Highway Department was back with plans to improve Main Street with curbs and gutters, sidewalks, turn lanes, and new lighting. Some of the townspeople objected, believing that such a major project in the heart of town would disrupt the visitors and endanger the income of many merchants. After months of argument, disagreement, and debate the town council finally gave approval to the project and in 1993 work was begun by the Highway Department. Two years later the work was finished, giving the town a new look.

At about the same time the building of a third park was undertaken, this time along the Red River itself in the heart of town. The library and museum projects at the east end of town were carried out and soon there began an ambitious program of beautification.

During these years the Chamber of Commerce was hard at work, always trying to promote more visitors and guests. A variety of special activities and events were undertaken and some of these proved so popular that they became a part of the Red River annual calendar. The oldest of these is the Aspencade Arts and Crafts

Show which has been a regular affair since 1971. It is traditionally held around the last week in September to coincide with the beautiful changing of the aspen leaves. The length of this celebration has varied from a single weekend to a full week and it has included square dancing and various entertainment in addition to the arts and crafts booths.

Memorial Day weekend is given over to the Red River Run, an annual motorcycle rally which began in 1982 and has grown to huge proportions. At this time the entire area is a gathering place for well over ten thousand cyclists who participate in various activities which include a special ceremony at the Vietnam Memorial in the Moreno Valley. A number of vendors set up in Red River and there is entertainment and special contests for the visitors.

In 1977, John Miller began the Annual Enchanted Circle Bike Tour which consists of a one hundred mile bicycle ride. Contestants begin their tour at the Town Hall and travel to Questa, Taos, then Angel Fire, Eagle Nest and over Bobcat Pass back into Red River. In 1988 the Top of the World Mountain Bike Race was added as part of the weekend activities. These events are usually held in early September and always draw a large number of cyclists.

Other special summer activities include the Big Oldies Car Show (an antique auto show) usually held in June and the Sportsman's Weekend with target bow hunting and fishing contests. The Women of the West Quilt Show is held annually the weekend following the Aspencade celebration.

The winter season opens at Thanksgiving with the opening of the ski area. There is a Community House party, preparations for the Christmas season and the first Torchlight Parade consisting of a number of skiers descending the face of the mountain carrying torches. The Christmas season has always been a time for many visitors and at this time there are a number of varied activities. A recent special winter activity is Mardi Gras in the Mountains which was first held in 1992. This week-long celebration is held just prior to Lent and includes parades, balls, outrageous costumes, food, and entertainment.

In 1995 the town of Red River held its centennial celebration. Over the preceding one hundred years much had transpired. The old mining town had given way to a place of summer visitors and this in turn had evolved into a year round resort. What had begun as a random collection of cabins, frame buildings, tents and sheds had been transformed into a large number of homes, condominiums, motels, lodges, resorts, restaurants, and shops. Although much remained of the old architectural look, there were now many new, different, and modern buildings. By this time the the people of Red River, like the rest of America, had adopted much of the trappings of the coming twenty-first century. They had become accustomed to television, recorded movies, fast foods, on-line shopping, personal telephones and had learned to designate new gadgets and devices by initials rather than by name: PC, SUV, GPS, ATV, VCR, CD, ATM, DVD, etc. It was now possible for the summer visitor to visit the library in the morning, collect and send e-mail, and still spend much of the day fishing one of the streams. Or one might spend the day climbing to one of the high lakes, and on return eat a gourmet meal, and later be entertained by a recent movie recorded on DVD.

Though much has changed, much remains the same. The near perfect summer weather continues to delight prairie land visitors who come to escape the heat. The brilliant whiteness of snow capped peaks still evokes the same awe and wonder. As always there are stunning cobalt skies, crystal clear tumbling streams, beautiful high mountain lakes, and glorious summer wildflowers. The deer, elk, bear, and beaver go about their lives as ever before and from all directions the beauty of nature beckons.

NOTES

Notes to Chapter One (PLACE)

1. The origin of the name Sangre de Christo (Blood of Christ) is obscure. William de Buys, in *Enchantment and Exploitation* has outlined several legends to explain the source of this name. The simplest and most likely is that the words derive from the reddish color of these mountains at sunset (the alpenglow).

2. This mountain was named for William Fraser, the leading mine developer in Amizette and Twining on the Rio Hondo. For reasons that are not clear the name appears as Frazer (with a "z") on many contemporary maps, including those of the National Geologic Survey and the Carson National Forest. One might guess that the error, once made, has simply been copied.

3. A fairly complete description of the flora of the Sangre de Christos can be found in an article by Paul J. Knight titled "The Flora of the Sangre de Christo Mountains" and found in *Tectonic Development of the Southern Sangro de Christo Mountains*. There is also an excellent book, *Meet the Natives* by M. Walter Pesman, which describes trees, shrubs, and flowers of the southern Rockies based on the various Life Zones. This book gives a clear understanding of these differing habitat zones.

4. Bob Prunty of Red River has kept meticulous precipitation records going back more than fifty years. A careful reading of these points out the wide variability of rainfall and snow. During the dry decade of the 1950s, precipitation averaged only 17 inches. The year 1957 saw just 11.64 inches but the following

year it rose to 26.84 only to fall the next year to 14.1. The decade of the nineties has been fairly wet in general with an above average precipitation of 23.6 inches. This decade was also an above average snow period with a yearly average of 196 inches.

5. The tale of Dawson is completely covered by Toby Smith in his book *Coal Town. The Life and Times of Dawson, New Mexico*. It makes for an interesting read; at least look at the pictures. The first mine was opened on the John B. Dawson ranch in the Vermejo Valley in 1899. It was purchased by Charles B. Eddy who began a large coal operation and brought in a railroad. In 1905 the property was bought by Phelps Dodge which built up and ran the company town down to the last detail. At its height, Dawson contained 6,000 people, three schools, two churches, a hospital, a large mercantile store, an Opera House, Gymnasium, and a public swimming pool. After World War II the mines were gradually closed, the town emptied of people, and then dismantled. What little remains now lies on private property leased to the CS Ranch.

Notes to Chapter Two
(PRELUDE)

1. One of the most well-known individuals to be incarcerated by Spain was Zebulon Pike of Pikes Peak fame. With two dozen men he set out to explore the headwaters of the Arkansas River. Becoming lost, the expedition wandered into the Rio Grande Valley and built a stockade on the Conejos River. The Spanish authorities, learning of its presence, ordered a company of dragoons to intercept the group and they were brought to Santa Fe. Subsequently the Americans were marched south to Chihuahua, then eastward to the border of Texas and released.

2. Much has been written about the Santa Fe Trail. William Hill's account, *The Santa Fe Trail, Yesterday and Today*, contains many pictures of points along the Trail as they appeared in the past as well as today. There are also illustrations of various wagons that were used to haul freight. Hill makes the point that the Santa Fe Trail was largely a commercial trail, unlike the Oregon and California Trails which were primarily for emigrants. It also served as a military invasion route used by Gen. Kearney during the Mexican-American War.

   Although most large caravans required about two months to make the journey, for men on horseback the time was much shorter. The speed record seems to have been set in 1848 by Francis X. Aubrey who, alone and on horseback, covered the distance in only six days.

3. One of the more interesting accounts of the Trail is Susan Magoffin's *Down the Santa Fe Trail and Into Mexico*. This young woman, of a wealthy and prominent Kentucky family, was married at the age of eighteen to Samuel Magoffin, a vet-

eran Santa Fe trader. In 1846 she accompanied her new husband on a trading trip over the Trail to Santa Fe and then south to Chihuahua, Mexico. This is her diary of the journey which is filled with details of the days on the trail as well as a description of the Santa Fe of that day. The trip occurred at the time of the Mexican-American War and they entered New Mexico coincident with the occupation by American troops.

Mrs. Magoffin's diary was handed down to her descendents and not published until 1926.

4. During the Eighteenth Century the French had explored, developed, and dominated the Mississippi Valley, claiming it for their own. At the Treaty of Paris in 1763 Spain was given the land west of the Mississippi, which was called the Louisiana Territory. The Spanish government adopted the custom of employing Frenchmen to administer this colony and this practice became commonplace. As a result there were many French immigrants to the area so that a considerable number of trappers, fur traders, and mountain men were of French descent.

The Territory was subsequently ceded to France and Napoleon promptly sold it to the United States in the famous Louisiana Purchase of 1803. This transaction more than doubled the size of the U.S.

5. Bent's Fort was a very imposing structure for its place and time. The walls were 14 feet high and 30 inches (or 3 adobe bricks) in thickness and there were two round towers for defense, 18 feet in height. Rooms faced inward toward a large courtyard or quadrangle with a timbered veranda all around. In addition to large storage areas there were 25 rooms each measuring 15 by 20 feet. Thus the fort was able to accommodate many people as well as a large amount of trade goods. It served as a favorite stopover on the Santa Fe Trail and a gathering

NOTES   211

   place for trappers, traders, and a variety of Indian tribes.
      Today the fort is located near La Junta, Colorado. It has
   been restored as accurately as possible and is a National Historic Site.

6. Charles Bent's house remains well preserved and is a historic landmark in Taos. Located on Bent Street one block north of the plaza, it is privately owned and is operated as a museum. Aside from the building itself there are items of historical interest related to Taos during the Nineteenth Century. It is well worth a visit.

7. The Sangre de Christo Grant (1,038,195 acres) was located north of Taos and extended from south of Costilla northward into Colorado beyond present day Fort Garland. Its western boundary was the Rio Grande and eastward it stretched to the high ridges of the Culebra Mountains. This included the Costilla, Culebra, and Trinchara watersheds as well as parts of the San Luis and Rio Grande Valleys. In the 1890s gold was discovered on La Belle Creek, a tributary of the Costilla and located only a few short miles from the Red River Valley.

   At the time when this grant was given, all of the land was included in the New Mexico Territory which belonged to Mexico. It was only later that the Colorado Territory (and state) was carved out and an arbitrary line established between New Mexico and Colorado. It is interesting that at one time a petition was made for a Mexican Land Grant covering an area that now is entirely located in the state of Colorado.

8. During his trapping days in the mountains Carson had married an Arapaho woman named Waa-nibe (Singing Wind), and the marriage eventually produced a daughter, Adaline. After the death of Waa-nibe in 1841, the care of his young daughter be-

came a matter of great concern to Kit. Realizing that his employment required long journeys and extensive absences, he struggled with the problem but was finally able to place her with his family in St. Louis.

When he contemplated marriage to Josefa, he was fearful that his half Indian daughter might be a hindrance to his acceptance by the proud and distinguished Jaramillo family. He sought advice from his future in-laws, the Bents, and apparently some type of solution was reached. Adaline was placed in a convent and Carson took the vows of the Catholic church.

Later, when Adaline became a young woman, Carson brought her to New Mexico. Here she met and married Louis Simmons.

9. I was unable to find the given name of St. Vrain's wife, the younger sister of Luz Beaubien. Lavender, in his book *Bent's Fort* (p. 429), researched this fairly carefully, including a search of the Taos parish records, but to no avail. I could find no subsequent information.

10. Visitors to the Gov. Bent House in Taos can see the hole dug into the adobe wall through which the women tried to make their escape. Also on display are the tongs and ladle used to break through.

    The Bent's daughter, Teresina, was five years old at the time of the slaying. Later in life and as a grown woman she wrote a short account of the events and a copy of this writing is available at the Bent House.

11. Simeon Turley had come to New Mexico in 1830. He established a distillery at Arroyo Hondo which became famous for its "Taos Lightning" a product known throughout the Southwest. He had developed a large establishment with a mill, gra-

NOTES

nary, stillhouse, and barns. The business employed both Mexicans and Indians from the surrounding area and served as a large market for grain raised in the Rio Hondo valley. During the rebellion Turley and nine of his men were besieged by a force of five hundred Indians and Mexicans. In spite of heavy attack the Americans were able to hold out for two days. Finally, the buildings were set ablaze, the attackers broke in, and Turley along with six of his men was killed. Three managed to escape and spread the word.

Today, the remains of Turley's distillery are located on private property at Arroyo Hondo.

12. I have presented only a summary of the events during the Taos uprising of 1847. Lavender, in *Bent's Fort,* describes in great detail this entire episode: the events leading up to the rebellion, the circumstances of Bent's death, the battles afterward, and the subsequent trial of the conspirators.

13. The western boundary of the Maxwell Land Grant was located along the mountain ridge above the Red River Valley and the grant extended eastward beyond the Canadian River. To the north it stretched into Colorado almost to Trinidad and its southern boundary lay south of Springer and Rayado Creek. It encompassed what is today the Moreno Valley, the Philmont Scout Ranch (135,000 acres), the Cimarron State Park, and the vast Vermejo Ranch (550,000 acres). It became home to a number of towns: Raton, Springer, Maxwell, Cimarron, Eagle Nest, and Angel Fire, as well as the ghost towns of Elizabethtown, Baldy Town, and Dawson. Today, if one drives from Bobcat Pass near Red River and travels almost to Trinidad the distance is close to 100 miles, all of it on Maxwell land.

The fascinating history of the grant is told in Jim Berry Pierson's book, *The Maxwell Land Grant.*

14. The Maxwell house is no longer standing, the remnants having been destroyed by fire in 1922. It was located just north of the present day St. James Hotel in Cimarron. Of all the Maxwell buildings the only one remaining is the Aztec Mill which today serves as the Old Mill Museum. The three-story building is very well preserved and contains a wealth of information as well as artifacts from the Maxwell family. In the below-ground floor can be seen part of the old machinery that was used to grind the grain.

Notes to Chapter Three
(GOLD FEVER)

1. In the early days some of the hardier souls would journey from Red River to Taos by taking the short cut directly over the mountains. The easiest route was by way of the Red River south to the Middlefork and then to the West Fork. By following that canyon upward about two miles one could cross the mountains in the vicinity of Bull of the Woods Meadow. From here, the trail dropped down to Twining (present day Taos Ski Area), and then followed the Rio Hondo out of the mountains and to Taos. An alternate route consisted of following Pioneer Creek to its source and then following the ridge over Gold Hill. From here one could journey south to Bull of the Woods Meadow or turn west and drop down into Long Canyon and then to Twining.

    Wagon Days in Red River tells of how Ed Westoby took the short cut over the mountains in order to deliver claims papers to Taos and beat out a rival claim jumper.

2. The richest mine in northern New Mexico was the Aztec, located on the eastern slopes of Baldy Mountain near the headwaters of Ute Creek. This mine was on the Maxwell Land Grant and its production of gold led to Lucien Maxwell becoming the wealthiest man in New Mexico. Later, the grant was sold by the Maxwells to an English consortium operating as the Maxwell Land Grant Company. In the 1890s, the Company reopened and expanded the mine in order to raise revenue. A hundred miners were hired, new tunnels were dug, and Baldy Town once again became a hive of activity with a population of 200 people. The St. Louis, Rocky Mountain, and Pacific Railroad laid track from Cimarron to Ute Park in order to serve the

Aztec. Plans were made to eventually extend the line further west to Elizabethtown and Taos but this never materialized.

Although the tracks have been removed, the old roadbed can easily be spotted along the highway between Ute Park and Cimarron. The old station at Ute Park has been demolished but was located just east of the present day post office. A large tunnel was dug to bypass the Eagle Nest Dam, and though the rail line was never built, the tunnel remains, high on the cliff side and south of the dam.

3. Evidence of mining activity along the West Fork of the Red River can still be seen today. There are collapsed mine tunnels and tailings piles along the Big Ditch not far from its origin at the West Fork. The old maps indicate these were claims by the Iron Dyke Group and the St. Louis Silver and Lead Co.

4. The Rock Island Company expressed interest in extending a line from Kansas through Maxwell City (Cimarron), up the Cimarron Canyon and eventually to Taos. There was also talk that the Union Pacific would extend its line from Trinidad to Vasquez on into the Taos area. In addition, there was hope that tracks would be extended from Embudo to Taos and into the Rio Hondo region. Of course, none of these schemes were ever accomplished.

5. Fraser Mountain (at 12,000 feet) looms above Middlefork Lake on its eastern side while the Taos Ski Area lies at its western base, a straight line distance of only about two miles. As pointed out in the second note to Chapter 1, the name is frequently misspelled on some current maps. The western, or Rio Hondo side of the mountain was heavily mined (mostly by Fraser), while the eastern, or Red River flank was never worked by prospectors.

NOTES

6. The population figures for the early mining camps are notoriously inaccurate. There was no official census and the numbers were rough estimates. Since almost no one possessed any kind of permanent address, the figures included visitors and transients as well as the residents; in addition, most counts included all those miners who might be living in tents or cabins in the surrounding vicinity even at some distance from the town. The greatest variable was the time of year when the estimate was made since a large number of the prospectors and miners left the mountains during the cold winter months and moved to warmer climates. This, of course, is the same situation we find in the area today when population numbers vary a great deal depending on the season. Imagine, if you will, making a rough estimate today of the number of people in the town of Red River on July Fourth and then repeating the exercise a few months later on December Fourth. There could be as much as a tenfold difference.

    By examining old photographs of the mining camps and noting the number of buildings, it seems clear that the number of permanent residents was much lower than some of the numbers that were advertised.

7. The site of Ditch Cabin, headquarters for the construction, is easily accessible today. It lies on the East Fork along Forest Trail 56 about one-half mile from the trailhead Where the trail crosses Sawmill Creek there is an open hillside which was the site of several building and it is not hard to make out a few level spots that mark old foundations. On the west side of the trail and along the creek was located the sawmill. A large excavation or pit marks the site of the waterwheel and there are a few remaining timbers. A short ditch diverted water from Sawmill Creek to power the wheel and there is also a ditch that brought

additional water from the East Fork. Several old roads led out of the area and some of these can still be followed.

8. There are almost no remaining records which might give us the details of the actual construction of the Big Ditch. Rossiter Raymond, in his report to the U.S. Secretary of Treasury, *Statistics of Mines and Mining in the States and Territories West of the Rocky Mountains* (1870), described portions of the ditch only two years after its construction but there is little mention of the problems and difficulties encountered during the building itself. There are two reports in the *Santa Fe New Mexican* written in the fall of 1868 which describe the project but both of these are short and rather incomplete. Davis, who was the superintendent of the endeavor, likely kept meticulous records and hopefully these may someday surface.

9. What remains of the Big Ditch can still be found throughout the upper Red River valley and in some places the ditch is surprisingly well preserved. In spite of forest encroachment, some filling by soil, humus, and rocks, in a number of spots it retains its original size and depth. The wooden flumes and trestles have long since fallen but in many places milled timbers can be found along with the old square nails. In a few locations (such as Foster Park and Fourth of July), the ditch was bulldozed to form a road bed.

One section that is still in good shape is found between the Old Red River Pass and Foster Park. Another is along the East Fork beyond Ditch Cabin where Forest Trail 56 crosses the Ditch.

Remnants of pipe from the Iron Flume are still to be found near the Old Red River Pass but are now on private property. A few sections of this iron pipe are on display at the Red River Museum.

NOTES 219

10. In 1906, the Big Ditch was purchased by the CS Cattle company, owned by the Springer brothers, Frank and Charles. Several years later the two men decided to build a dam at the mouth of the Moreno Valley to impound water for the irrigation of property near Cimarron. Land was purchased from the Maxwell Land Grant Company and construction was begun in 1916. Eagle Nest Dam was finally completed in 1920, forming Eagle Nest Lake.

    In 1939, the C S Cattle Co. petitioned the New Mexico State Engineer for a permit to reopen the Big Ditch as a means of increasing water flow into Eagle Nest Lake and thus into the Cimarron River. The request was denied on the basis that the ditch had not been in use for many years and therefore all water rights had lapsed. At the time of the petition, a survey of the Ditch was carried out and it is on file at the Office of State Engineer (No. 0848).

11. William Gallagher, one of the sons of Charles Gallagher and Mae Lowrey Gallagher, married Laurelle Errington and continued to operate the ranch. Their son, Joseph Gallagher, following a stint in the newspaper business in California, returned to the Moreno Valley in 1973 and shortly thereafter launched the *Sangre de Christo Chronicle*.

12. The town of Catskill had developed as the result of efforts by the Maxwell Land Grant Company to exploit the large timber reserves on its property. The Denver, Texas, and Fort Worth Railroad had been persuaded to extend track from Trinidad, Colo. to Catskill and the town had grown up as the hub for an active timber industry. When a decent road was opened to La Belle, this route provided easy transportation from La Belle to Trinidad and points beyond.

In 1894 the railroad fare from Trinidad to Catskill was a dollar and ten cents and the stage fare from Catskill to La Belle five dollars. Thus one might travel from Trinidad to La Belle in a single day at a cost of only $6.10.

13. Winnie Hamilton, in her *Wagon Days in Red River,* tells of a small group of young men who would ride into La Belle for the dances. They were mounted on fine horses, seemed flush with money, and were well mannered. After spending a short time in town they would attend the dancing and entertain the young ladies, following which the group would disappear only to return weeks or months later. At a later time it was discovered that these men were the notorious Black Jack Ketchum and his gang of outlaws.

    Ketchum and his brother had a ranch in the Valle Vidal located not far from La Belle and this served as one of their many hideouts. Ketchum was eventually captured and taken to the town of Clayton where he was hung. The story is told that on the day before his execution the gallows was built and then tested with a weighted sack. Unfortunately, someone forgot to remove the weight which hung all night long, stretching and stiffening the rope. At the time of Ketchum's hanging, the rope had no elasticity and pulled his head off--or as a local observer noted, "it popped it plumb off".

14. At the present time the site of La Belle lies in the Valle Vidal Unit of the Carson National Forest and can only be reached on foot. It is only two miles off Forest Road 1950 at the point where the road leaves Comanche Creek and turns north (at the trail to Clayton Camp). From here one can easily walk the two miles to La Belle partly following the old stage route.

    The La Belle hunting lodge sits almost in the forest and faces eastward toward the old townsite.

Notes to Chapter Four
(RED RIVER CITY)

1. Two of the original Mallette cabins still stand and are now listed on the National Register of Historic Places. The Orin Mallette house is currently located on the River Ranch property at the west end of town. The Sylvester Mallette cabin was originally located in the eastern part of town near the Westoby cabin. When the town was platted, it had to be moved and was relocated to its present place on the Prunty property at the northwest corner of Copper King and River Street.

2. A complete and interesting account of the Young family can be found in the fourth *Historical Souvenir Guide* published by the *Red River Miner* in 1998. There is an accompanying picture of B. J. and Sara along with eleven of their children taken when most of the family was grown.

    The Young house came to be located at 600 E. Main and remained in place until the early 1990s when it was demolished. A couple of the pink bricks (made at the brickyard on Orin Mallette's land) which were salvaged can now be seen in the Red River Museum.

3. Five generations of Brandenburgs have graced the town of Red River and all of them have played a role in its story. Detailed information about this entire family has been described by Alyce Densow and can be found in her columns in the *Red River Miner* in July of 2000.

4. Laura Krehbiel, in *Red River New Mexico, Your Mountain Playground,* quotes an old-timer's description of coming into the town: "When we came over the hill into Red River we had

to tie a big tree on the back to hold the brake of the wagon. One man drove and the other rode the brakes and another watched the tree. We women and the children walked. It took us from nine o'clock in the morning until three o'clock in the afternoon to get from the top of the hill to the bottom, into Red River Valley."

In *Wagon Days in Red River,* Winnie Hamilton relates the story of the first automobile to make a journey down the Big Hill. It was an Overland car driven by a man from Raton named Kirshner. A tree was chained to the back of the auto and chains were placed on all four wheels. By applying full brakes, the car was able to descend slowly and successfully. On the return trip up the pass the car had to be pulled by a team of horses.

5. F. Stanley, in *The Red River, New Mexico Story* lists a roster of the school's students, made when the school had been in existence several years, i.e., some time in the early 1900s. At the time L. W. Brown was teacher. There were six Youngs (Muriel, Stella, Mamie, Lulu, Jessie, Earl), four Hattons (Willis, Ernest, Agnes, Ida), four children named Phipps (Bessie, Bert, Lulu, Charlie), two Brandenburgs (Charlotte, John) and one Mallette (Beulah). There were also four McCollums (Mabel, Wilfred, Dave, Jesse) and three students named Putnam (Horace, Roxie, Alta).

6. Many of the mines in Pioneer canyon can still be seen today. The Carson National Forest has produced a brochure indicating the location of the Ajax, Stella, and Inferno as well as later mines such as the Smith property, Moberg claims, the Crowe, and Caribel. These are along Pioneer Road which begins near the Ski Area and extends several miles up Pioneer Canyon to the Caribel.

NOTES

7. Edward Westoby was born in England in 1863 and came to the United States at age 16. He worked at several different occupations and after coming West made his living as a trapper. He appeared in Red River soon after the Mallettes and lived here for over forty years. The Westoby cabin, located near the eastern end of town at High St. and Jay Hawk Tr., still stands today. Adjacent to the cabin is the old Miners' Hospital which Westoby moved to this site after the Hospital was abandoned. He and his wife, Margaret, used this building as their home.

   Like many of the early settlers, Westoby remained a jack-of-all-trades: in addition to being a trapper and prospector, he was an accomplished taxidermist as well as a writer, and for a time he served as deputy sheriff. One of his most noted accomplishments was the discovery of the Moly Mine.

8. Parts of the Oldham buildings still remain and can be reached from the Placer Creek Road (road to Goose Lake). The remains of the cabin can be easily located and face eastward toward a pretty meadow. The "Unfinished Cabin" was to have been an assay office but was never completed; it is surprisingly well preserved. From the collapsed tunnel of the Golden Treasure a small stream of water trickles forth, a reminder of the mine's flooding. Above and to the west of the cabin is the site and remains of the water wheel, still present after a hundred years. Look for the ditch which brought water from Goose Creek.

   The Carson National Forest has prepared an interpretive brochure of the various mines along Placer Creek. Many of the mines are marked with sign posts and they can be found along the Placer Creek jeep road.

9. Tom Gill built his cabin in Goose Creek canyon and located it high on a shelf several hundred feet above the creek itself. The

building was actually reached by a wagon road that followed the East Fork of Placer Creek and then wound around and over the ridge into Goose Creek canyon. The cabin was located in a grove of giant aspens, had a sod roof, and was well known for its picturesque appearance and beautiful location. Walter Hamilton would tell about Tom's still, which was located behind the cabin and was the source of local whiskey. It seems that a bear broke into the still, consumed too much liquor, and "raised quite a ruckus" with the still. The bear finally fell asleep and after several hours awakened and wandered off

10. This toll road began at the junction of the East and West Forks of Placer and extended over the mountain at today's Ski Area in the vicinity of the Kit Carson ski run. It came down into Red River at the present location of the main lift house.

11. The stamp mill at Black Copper still stands today after a hundred years and is thought to be the only surviving mill of its kind in New Mexico. The stamps consist of heavy pistons attached to a shaft which was turned by a large wheel. As the wheel rotated the pistons were raised several feet in the air and then allowed to fall onto the ore, crushing it to a fine powder. This was then washed through sluice boxes lined with mercury plates. In this way much of the gold could be recovered although it still required smelting to remove all impurities.

   The mine shaft at Black Copper has been capped for safety reasons but extends to a depth of 250 feet and there are five different levels.

   The mine and stamp mill are now listed on the National Register of Historic Places. The property is owned by Ina Siler of Oklahoma City.

NOTES 225

12. The smelter was located at the mouth of Pioneer Canyon near the present-day site of the main chair lift.

13. The June Bug Mill was built just west of town in the vicinity of today's June Bug Campground. (The June Bug *mine* was located about four miles up Bitter Creek).

14. The problems and costs of hauling the ore can be illustrated by a story told by Winnie Hamilton in *Wagon Days in Red River*. The story concerns Grandpa Bob Pooler, a partner in the Memphis mine. "Grandpa Pooler sacked up two tons of high grade ore and hauled it by wagon to Red River and on to Pueblo. He received $80.00 a ton for it, but by the time he took his expenses out for the long trip in freighting, he was broke and had to write for $100.00 to make the return trip back home."

15. A ball mill consisted of a hollow steel cylinder 8 to 10 feet long and 4 to 6 feet in diameter. Ore was placed into the drum along with a number of steel balls, four inches in diameter. The cylinder was then rotated and after a number of hours the ore would be ground to a fine powder.

    There are several of these steel balls on display in the Red River Museum.

16. In chapter 3, the section on La Belle, the history of the Sangre de Christo Grant is outlined. The Costilla Estate belonged to a Dutch company, the US Freehold and Emigration Company. It is obvious today that the watershed of Bitter Creek did not lie on the Sangre de Christo Land Grant property, but the Independence Mine is only about one mile from the boundary line and in those days there were few accurate maps.

17. Like many of the early miners, Scarvarda had a rather colorful

history. He was born in Costellamonte, Italy in 1863 and given the name of Luigi Vitorrio Scarvarda. He came to the US at age fifteen and changed his name to Louis Victor. On his arrival he wound up in Austin, Texas where he worked on the building of the State Capitol. After a time spent in St. Louis, Scarvarda moved to Starkville, Colo. and opened a saloon. Besides his other ventures (general store, packing house, ranch), he built and operated a Macaroni factory. He caught the "gold bug" in 1904, bought his claims, and worked at them for twenty-four years.

18. At the Big Five (Orofino) Mine just south of Anchor some of the original equipment remains today. There is a large steam boiler and steam hoist located just west of the trail and on the hillside. Two shafts remain along with the remnants of the water wheel, and there is a cabin on the east side of the stream.

19. Some of the remnants of the Crowe cabin still stand and are marked by a Forest Service signpost. Careful inspection will show what remains of the rock garden just south of the cabin even though the creek has formed a new channel and no longer flows through the garden.

20. The Caribel was dismantled in the 1980s and all the machinery removed. The large separator wheel used in the mill is now located at the Red River Museum.

21. The Moly Mine has now been in production for about eighty years. Early on much of the work was surface mining but for many years now the work has been deep underground with the vertical depth at about 1200 feet. A large adit tunnel extends from the vicinity of the mill a distance of one mile to connect with the lower levels of the mine. At present the Moly Corp. conducts visitor tours deep into the mine.

Notes to Chapter Five
(TRANSITION)

1. Years later Kenneth Balcomb wrote a book, *The Red River Hill,* in which he relates his adventures building the Red River Pass Road. He describes in detail how the construction was carried out and some of the problems that were met. The supervisory group stayed at the Penn Hotel in Red River, next door to the H. L. Pratt home (Pratt was operator of the Caribel Mine). Balcomb gives a very interesting description of life in the town at that time and he writes about some of the people.

2. In *The Red River Hill,* Balcomb describes a hair-raising event involving Wheatcroft. One morning as his team of four horses was pulling the plow, the right hand (or downhill) horse fell onto its side and began to slide backwards down the slope, held back only by the harness attached to the other horses. To say the least, the rest of the team were terrified as were the bystanders who expected all the horses to be pulled down the mountainside and killed. Yelling and swearing, Wheatcroft was able to calm and sooth all the horses. Taking a heavy rope from the plow handle, he managed to slowly place it around the chest of the fallen horse and then attach it to the other horses. After disconnecting the harness, he was then able to turn the downed horse around so that its feet were pointing downhill. With a great deal of effort and loud words, he then got the horse back on its feet. After a short rest (the entire episode took four hours), to everyone's amazement, Wheatcroft hitched up his team and resumed plowing.

3. For a number of years Walter Hamilton led summer visitors on horseback trips into the high country. He knew intimately all of

the trails, byways, and out of the way places in the surrounding mountains.

Presumably because of her girlhood ambition to be an actress, Winnie from time to time would play the role of "Rosie", a flashy woman with a painted face and wearing flamboyant clothes. She might suddenly appear in this guise in meetings, at restaurants, and before her summer visitors. Those unacquainted with Rosie might never guess that this unusual character was actually Winnie Hamilton.

4. Winnie Hamilton was the first native of Red River to compile any kind of historical account of the area. Her first book, *Wagon Days in Red River,* was written in 1946 and is still a good source for events during the first half of the Twentieth Century. Because of her influence, others were encouraged to write, either memoirs or other articles about the town's history, thereby leading to the collection of historical information that we have today.

5. In 2001, Alyce Densow wrote an article about the Young family which appeared in the *Red River Miner.* She quoted some interesting prices found on a menu from the 1950s that was used in the Young's Ranch restaurant:
    eggs and ham - 85 cents
    sandwiches - 50 to 85 cents
    chicken fried steak - $1.85
    lobster tail - $2.50
    coffee, tea, milk - 10 cents
    hot cereal - 10 cents
    two pork chops - $1.85

6. This building is still owned by fourth generation Brandenburgs, J. D. and his wife Renay. It houses the Red River Mining Co.

NOTES

(a liquor store), movie rental, and a pub.

7. When Lottie became postmistress there was jealousy and opposition to her on the part of several of those in the community. She had intended to move the post office from its location at High St. and Mallette to a new location on High St. (behind the present Red River Inn). Before the move could be made this new building was blown up with dynamite. The certain identity of the culprits was never proven though suspicions were strong. Subsequently, Lottie moved the post office to a different location, still on High St. but across from today's William's Trading Post.

8. In October of 1940 there appeared in the *New Mexico Magazine* an article about Joe Cannard written by Grace Ray. In a very interesting way the author captured the character of the old prospector, hunter, guide and all around mountain man. In an interview, Cannard claimed the record for slaying the largest grizzly bear ever killed in New Mexico--weighing in at 1,200 pounds. The hide, which weighed 61 pounds, sold for $65.

9. One of Aunt Becky's favorite stories which she liked to tell on herself had to do with an early trip into Red River. It seems her party was coming down the very steep Big Hill and a heavy log was chained to the wagon. Only the driver and brakeman remained with the wagon, all others walked. Halfway down, the wagon overturned and all the belongings went flying down the steep hill. Looking down, the group decided that Becky's empty suitcase was suspended high in a tree. When they got close enough to see, there was no suitcase, only two pair of Becky's white, ruffled panties waving in the breeze for all to see.

10. When the Little Red School House was moved to its present location and became home to the Red River Museum, a plot

was set aside to recreate Aunt Becky's garden. This is planted with many of the same flowers which she grew--delphinia, columbine, poppies, pansies.

11. L. S. Lewis' all purpose tractor was kept by the Lewis family and could be found at Brett's Steakhouse, owned and operated by Brett Lewis.

12. Lester's classmates at the Red River School included Herbert Pratt, Shirley, Alberta, and Patsy Phipps, Johnny and Bud Gallagher, Tony Simion, Jr., and Johnny Brandenburg.

13. Opal Guinn and the Gallagher-Guinn stable received a featured write-up in the *Red River Colossal* in April of 1947.

14. In the July 4, 2000 Historical Edition of the *Red River Miner*, Tamara Jo Gallagher Arvila describes growing up in the Gallagher cabin in Mallette Canyon. It would be considered crude and rough by today's standards but was very typical of most all the dwelling places in Red River before 1940. Water was drawn from a nearby spring and there was no indoor plumbing or bathroom, only a non-heated outhouse. The cabin contained a wood stove for both heating and cooking. For a time kerosene lanterns were used for light but later an electric generator was installed.

    In spite of conditions which some today would consider as hardships, the Gallagher family seemed to thoroughly enjoy their summers in the mountains.

15. John Brandenburg has outlined how the local gamblers would evade the lawmen. A system was in place to give warning ahead of time and when a raid was expected, the slot machines, tables, and other equipment would suddenly disappear.

NOTES 231

By the time the law officers raced into town, the bars would be quiet and clean with one or two couples dancing to soft music. The bartender would have on a fresh shirt and would already be setting up a round of drinks on the house. After a while, during which the deputies were assured that no gaming was going on, the officers would pile into their cars and return to Taos. Before they had reached Questa, the gambling equipment would have been broken out again and the action would be in full swing. (Brandenburg composed a short article describing the gambling days and this write-up is on file at the Red River Museum).

16. The Red River Museum contains a good many artifacts from the Simion family including several items from Tillie's political years. There are also a couple of pieces of gambling equipment from Tony's Bar.

17. A good description of the annual ice harvest is outlined by Winnie Hamilton in *Reflections from Raton to Red River* (the pictures are worth a look). Winnie owned and displayed one of the six foot ice saws in her museum in the Melson cabin. John Brandenburg has also given us a picture of the ice harvest and his write-up is among the Red River Historical Society papers.

18. The volunteer workers that first summer included:
 from Wichita Falls - Claude Young, Earl Lowrance, Ted
  Harris, Hal Yeager, Fred Cone
 from Enid - Ike Crawford, Waldo Poor
 from Aspermont - C. Spect, Jack Chambless
 from Amarillo - Mel Barkley
 from Chattanooga, Oklahoma - Mont Dalton
 from Kansas City - Bob Fizzel
 from Red River - Clifton Lewis

19. Ruth Yeager served as president of the Community House Committee for the first ten years and most of the credit for its success should go to her. In 1977 she wrote a short book titled *The Red River Community House* and here she described the entire adventure of its conception, birth and growth.

20. In *Reflections from Raton to Red River* Winnie Hamilton describes in some detail the early phone service. For some strange reason the Hamiltons were sometimes able to pick up phone conversations via her radio and thus there was really no privacy on the line.

21. It was at the Monte Vista Lodge that Rosie Frambers met another summer guest, Henrietta Jones, who later married Johnny Mutz. The two couples remained lifelong friends.

Notes to Chapter Six
(YEAR ROUND RESORT)

1. The agreement between the Boltons and Carson National Forest stated that the improvements would consist of the following: chair lifts, T-bar lifts, J-bar lifts and similar devices; lunch room or restaurant; sale and rental of ski and other winter sports equipment; ski shop; ski instruction; first aid and ski patrol room; parking area; sanitation facilities; water supply; utilities; communication system; ski slopes and trails; snack bar and warming shelter at upper terminus of chair lifts; snack bar and warming shelter at lower terminus of lifts.

2. Some have claimed that Stokes Bolton did more for the town of Red River than anyone else and in many ways this is hard to refute. The building of the Ski Area changed the town completely, creating many new possibilities and opening up a new future. It laid the ground work for the town we know today.

    Stokes was not only a man of vision, he possessed the ability and drive to turn his visions into reality. Incidentally, both he and Audrey were accomplished pilots and owned their own plane.

3. It seems that Gary Starbuck was an expert at snowmaking and with the ample equipment owned by the Powder Puff this ski area was usually ready for skiing long before the other resorts. The claim was made that it was frequently the first ski area in the nation to open the season.

4. Because of his great interest in exploring and hiking and his many years in the area, John Miller knows more about the

back country than anyone else. In addition to being familiar with all the well-known trails he likes to talk about his list of "Ten little known routes and seldom taken hikes around Red River". These include Relica Peak, Miller Falls, Pioneer Lake, Fossil Cliffs, Hottentot Wash, and Wheeler Peak via the Tepee.

5. The Old Pass Road is open today and can easily be driven. At the east end of town take the highway to the right (578) and proceed south about one mile. Just before reaching Tall Pine Resort the Pass Road leads to the left and is marked by a sign. The Forest Service recommends 4-wheel drive which is not necessary going up but is handy on the descent where it will save on the brakes. The distance to the top is about three miles and some of the views from the mountainside are truly spectacular. At the top climb the hill to the north and get a rare view of the town of Red River. Directly to the west is the long Goose Creek canyon leading up to Gold Hill and to the southwest are Wheeler Peak and Fraser Mountain.

6. Through the years a number of Red River citizens have performed in the Wild West Melodrama show. In July of 2001, Alyce Densow wrote a series of articles for the *Red River Miner* about the Frye and Bowser families. In an interview for the article, Lovilla Bowser listed some of the townspeople who had taken part in putting on the production These included: Shelby Dawson, Wayne Kidd, Randall Kiker, Billy Addison, John Gill, Christine Jordan, Mike Nolan, Justin Brandenburg, Cliff Johnson, Cade Brown, Bill Hubbard, and Frank Venaglia.

In a July, 1974 issue of the *Red River Prospector* there is a picture depicting some of the melodrama action. Lovilla Bowser is shown in the role of Annabelle.

7. Don and Francis lived immediately behind the Trading Post

NOTES

and there Don would feed a variety of animals. He arranged several bird feeders plus a large table on which he kept deer corn. As a result a large herd of deer would come down off Flaggie mountain almost daily. Don bragged about how much money he spent on his animal friends - about $60 a week.

8. In the July 18, 1991 issue of the *Sangre de Christo Chronicle* there appeared an article about the Allens. In an interview Letha recalled an incident which occurred in the early years. It seems that a family came in to inquire about lodging and asked how high it was. Letha, assuming they were asking about the altitude replied, "It's eighty-seven fifty." Things got real quiet until she realized that the people were actually asking about cost. She was able to reassure them that the room price was actually $9.

9. Originally, dues were $3 per year. This fee was later raised to $5 and then in the 1990s to $10 annually.

10. The actual ownership of the Little Red School House remained in doubt until 1981 when the District Judge awarded custody to the Questa School District. It remained in their hands until 1998 when the Town of Red River purchased it for $36,000. The building was renovated and moved to its present location alongside the Library and it now houses the Red River Museum.

    In 1984 the Little Red School House was placed on the National Registry of Historic Places.

11. The number of locals who worked the Ski Area at one time or another is surprising large. In 1990 the *Sangre de Christo Chronicle* ran an article and paid tribute to all the folks who had been employees. The long list of names included Mutz, Miller, Young, Prunty, Mayer, Stephens, Brunson, Judycki,

Tweed, Simion, Lamb, Brandenburg, Buchanan, Burnham, Pockrandt, Hoag, Snead, Stahman, Klein, Coss, and Hatch.

12. Many of the Red River townspeople are forced to work at a second (or even third) job. Over the years, Texas Red's has employed many part-time people so that the list of its "alumni" is extensive.

13. Near their home on the East Fork the Russell's built a beautiful small lake which has subsequently been known as Russell's Pond. It can be found by following Highway 578 through the Upper Valley to the end of the pavement, then left over the bridge. Here turn to the right on the main road and follow south for only a short distance.

14. Maxine Taylor lost her first husband and subsequently married Bill Grindstaff. Both were missionaries and school teachers and Bill served as pastor to the First Baptist Church of Questa. In 1976 Maxine was awarded the New Mexico Mother of the Year Award and not long after was named America's Mother of the Year. She traveled to Washington, D.C. and was given the award by President Gerald Ford.

15. The Prunty building has served in several capacities and still contains the old post office boxes used during the time of Bob's being postmaster.

Notes to Chapter Seven
(INCORPORATION)

1. This was not the first or the last time that an event of this type occurred in the history of Red River. On occasion, a new idea or plan would be proposed and then would be met with considerable opposition. After a time the townspeople would come together and all would be worked out.

2. Drew Judycki came west to New Mexico and was attracted to Red River where he worked at the ski area, becoming ski school supervisor in 1966. In 1984 when the ski area was up for sale Drew became a part of the Red River Ski Area Corporation, the group which became the new owners. He served as vice-president and general manager for the ski area and in the nineties bought out his other partners so that he and his wife Susie became owners of the corporation.

3. Other members of the board were: Tillie Simion as vice-president, Judy Brunson, secretary, and treasurer Sheryl Snead. In addition Kitty Veale was made the acquisitions librarian and Ken Densow was to be liason person with the town.

4. The next time you enter the Red River Library, search for the portrait of Fanny Bliss. She would be proud of what her efforts have wrought.

5. Other original directors of the Historical Society were: Winnie Hamilton, Florence Oldham, Tillie Simeon, John Brandenburg, John Miller, Dora Lou Hickam, and Henrietta Mutz.

6. A brief perusal of Appendix A will reveal the great contribution

of Alyce Densow in collecting histories of many families and individuals. Under her by-line have appeared articles concerning such names as: Brandenburg, Buchanan, Fisher, Frye, Bowser, Hamilton, Lewis, Maroney, Miller, Simion, Tompkins, Young, Williams, and Woerndle.

7. To Fritz Davis goes much credit for his promotion of Red River's colorful past. Because of his own interest in history Fritz has become very knowledgeable about the early people and events in the life of the town. Using the *Red River Miner* he has been able to share that knowledge with all the people of the community.

8. As previoiusly noted in Note 4 of Chapter Five, Winnie Hamilton, more than anyone else, was responsible for the preservation of much of Red River's history. She published two different books describing some of the early events and people, and established a Museum in the old Melson cabin on Tall Pine property. She was also active in the R. R. Historical Society. Winnie set the tone and became the role model for preserving the area's history and she inspired others to follow in her footsteps.

APPENDIX A

Sources for additional information on some of the Red River families and people:

Allen, Terry and Letha -
    Article in *Sangre de Christo Chronicle*, July, 1991.

Bolton, Stokes and Audrey -
    Article in *Red River Miner*, January, 1995.
    Red River Historical Society files - Ski Area file.

Brandenburg family -
    Red River Miner, July 4, 2000 Historical Edition.
    Series of articles by Alyce Densow, *Red River Miner*, June 29, July 6, July 13, 2000.
    Taos El Crepusculo, April 1, 1954 - article written about Lottie Brandenburg at the time of her retirement as Postmaster.
    Red River Historical Society files: notes and articles, some written by John Brandenburg.
    Red River Miner, Fourth Historical Souvenir Guide.

Brunson family -
    There is a general display of the Brunson family in the Red River Museum.
    Red River Historical Society files.

Buchanan family -
    Article in *Red River Miner*, March 16, 2000, written by Alyce Densow.

Calhoun family -
>   *Sangre de Christo Chronicle*, June, 1990 - article about Glen and the Superette plus Der Markt, Ted and Beth Calhoun.

Coffelt, Rebecca - "Aunt Becky" -
>   Article appearing in the *Sangre de Christo Chronicle*, October 3, 1985.
>   Krehbiel, Laura, *Red River New Mexico, Your Mountain Playground*. Clayton, NM: Laura Krehbiel, 1939.
>   Article by Vernon Hendry in *Red River Colossal*, July, 1947.
>   Red River Historical Society files: various notes.

Densow, Alyce and Ken -
>   *Red River Miner* - article appearing in the July 20, 2000 issue.
>   There is an article in the *Sangre de Christo Chronicle*, of August 15, 1991.
>   *Red River Miner* - article written at the time of Ken's death, October 12, 2000.

Fisher, Bud and Betty -
>   *Red River Miner* - A couple of articles written by Alyce Densow. May 24 and May 31, 2001.

Frye - Bowser family -
>   *Red River Miner* articles by Alyce Densow: July 12, July 19, July 26, 2001.
>   *Red River Prospector*, July, 1974, article and picture of Frye's "shoot-out" at Old Town.

Gallagher family -
>   *Red River Miner*, Historical Edition, July 4, 2000.
>   Article in the *Red River Colossal*, April, 1947.

APPENDIX A   241

   Moreno Valley Writers Guild, *Lure, Lore and Legends of the Moreno Valley*. Angel Fire, NM: Columbine Pub. Group, 1997.
   Red River Miner, Fourth Historical Souvenir Guide.

Gill family -
   Sangre de Christo Chronicle, December, 1987. Story about the Gills and a short history of Texas Reds.

Hamilton, Walter and Winifred -
   Red River Miner, January 22, 1998 - article at Winnie's death.
   Taos News, January 22, 1998 - at Winnie's death.
   Hamilton, Winifred, *Wagon Days in Red River*, 1947.
   Red River Historical Society files: misc. notes and records.
   Hamilton, Winifred, *Reflections from Raton to Red River*. 1991.
   Krehbiel, Laura, *Red River, New Mexico, Your Mountain Playground*. Clayton, NM: Laura Krehbiel, 1939.
   Red River Miner, article titled, "Tall Pine Resort" by Alyce Densow, March 24, 2002.

Lewis family -
   Articles by Alyce Densow, *Red River Miner*, August 17, August 24, August 31, 2000.
   Red River Miner, July 4, 2000 Historical Edition.
   Red River Museum: display pictures and information.

Mallette brothers -
   Red River Miner, Fourth Historical Souvenir Guide.
   Pierson, Jim Berry, *The Red River - Twining Area: A New Mexico Mining Story*. Albuquerque: Univ. of New Mexico Press, 1986.

Hamilton, Winifred, *Wagon Days in Red River*, 1947.
Red River Historical Society files: notes by John Brandenburg; nomination forms of the Mallette Cabins for the National Register of Historic Places.

Maroney - Harold and Tinkie
Red River Miner - three separate articles by Alyce Densow, Sept. 7, Sept.14, Sept. 21, 2000.

Miller family -
Red River Miner - Alyce Densow wrote a series of articles for the issues of November 9, 16, 23, 30, the year 2000.
Sangre de Christo Chronicle, August 29, 1991. Describes the Powderpuff, Cross Country Skiing, various businesses.

Mutz family -
Winter Enchantment, *Working It Out on a Ranch*,1990.
Moreno Valley Writers Guild, *Lure, Lore and Legends of the Moreno Valley*. Angel Fire, NM:Columbine Pub. Group, 1997
Red River Historical Society files: various notes.

Oldham brothers -
Pierson, Jim Berry, *The Red River - Twining Area: A New Mexico Mining Story*. Albuquerque: Univ. of New Mexico Press, 1986.
Hamilton, Winifred,*Wagon Days in Red River*, 1947.
Red River Historical Society files: nomination of the Melson cabin for the National Register of Historic Places.

Phipps family -
Red River Miner, Fourth Historical Souvenir Guide.

APPENDIX A   243

    Moreno Valley Writers Guild, *Lure, Lore and Legends of the Moreno Valley*. Angel Fire, NM: Columbine Pub. Group, 1997.

Prunty family -
    Red River Miner, March 2, 2000.
    Red River Miner, November 22, 2001.

Simion family -
    Simion, Tillie, edited by Judy Wallner, *Tillie: An American Life*. 1981.
    Red River Museum: display and items.
    Article in *Taos News*, July 9, 1964.
    Red River Historical Society files: numerous articles, notes, Tillie's scrapbook.
    Articles in the *Red River Miner* by Alyce Densow, April 4, April 11, 2002.

Tompkins - Ann and Mel
    Red River Miner - Feb.1, Feb.8, 2001. A couple of articles by Alyce Densow.

Young family -
    Red River Miner, Fourth Historical Souvenir Guide.
    Red River Museum: display
    Red River Historical Society files: notes, articles.
    Series of articles by Alyce Densow in the *Red River Miner*, June 21, June 28, July 5, 2001.

Williams, Don and Frances -
    Red River Miner - May 11, 18, 22, June 8, 15, all in the year 2000. A series of writings by Alyce Densow.

Woerndle family -
> *Red River Miner* - reports in the issues of July 27, August 3, August 10 by Alyce Densow.
> *Sangre de Christo Chronicle* - Jan. 11, 1990. The thirtieth anniversary of the Red River Ski Area.

APPENDIX B

Red River Postmasters -
1. B. J. Young - around 1900
2. R. W. Penn - early 1900s
3. C. C. Clapper - early 1900s
4. Horace "Cap" Johnson - 1923 - 1934
5. Lottie Brandenburg - 1934 - 1954
6. Bette Simion - 1954 - 1957
7. Bob Prunty - 1957 - 1985
8. Joe Carrier - 1985 - 2002

Red River Mayors -
1. David Stults - 1971 -76
2. Ted Calhoun - 1976 - 78
3. John Miller - 1978 - 86
4. Harold Young - 1986 - 90
5. John Saint - 1990 -91
6. Alan Buchanan - 1991 - 92
7. John Tillery - 1992 - 1998
8. Craig Swagerty - 1998 -

BIBLIOGRAPHY

Balcomb, Kenneth C. *The Red River Hill*. Albuquerque, NM: Albuquerque Historical Society,1981.
Bauer, Paul W. "Elizabethtown" in *Tectonic Development of the Southern Sangre de Christo Mountains*. Socorro, NM: New Mexico Geological Society, 1976.
Bauer, Paul W. "The Big Ditch" in *Tectonic Development of the Southern Sangre de Christo Mountains*. Socorro, NM, New Mexico Geological Society, 1990.
Beck, Warren. *New Mexico. A History of Four Centuries*. Norman, OK: Univ. of Oklahoma Press, 1962.
Boyer, Jeffrey L. "The Black Copper Mine: Archeological Survey Near Red River, Taos County," New Mexico. *Archeology Notes No. 40*. Santa Fe: Museum of New Mexico, 1991.
Christiansen, Paige. *The Story of Mining in New Mexico*. Socorro, NM: New Mexico Bureau of Mines and Mineral Resources.
Claussen, W. E. "There Was Gold in Every Gulch", *New Mexico Magazine*, April, 1948.
Cottrell, Steve. *Civil War in Texas and New Mexico Territory*. Gretna, LA: Pelican Publishing Company, 1998.
Crutchfield, James. *Tragedy at Taos: The Revolt of 1847*. Plano, Texas: Republic of Texas Press.
Dreem, Stella M., ed. *Down the Santa Fe Trail and Into Mexico. The Diary of Susan Shelly Magoffin. 1846-1847*. Lincoln, Nebraska: Univ. of Nebraska Press., 1926.
Garrard, Lewis. *Wah-to-yah and the Taos Trail*. Norman, OK: Univ. of Oklahoma Press, 1955.
Gowans, Fred R.. *Rocky Mountain Rendezvous*. Layton, Utah: Gibbs-Smith Press,1985.

BIBLIOGRAPHY

Guild, Thelma S. and Harvey L. Carter. *Kit Carson. A Pattern for Heroes*. Lincoln, Neb.: Univ. of Nebraska Press, 1984.

Hamilton, Winifred O. *Reflections from Raton to Red River*. W.O. Hamilton, 1991.

Hamilton, Winifred O. *Wagon Days in Red River*. W. O. Hamilton, 1947.

Hill, William E. *The Santa Fe Trail Yesterday and Today*. Caldwell, Idaho: Caxton Printers, 1992.

Hilton, Tom. *Nevermore, Cimarron, Nevermore*. Ft. Worth, TX: Western Heritage Press, 1970.

Jones, F. A. *New Mexico Mines and Minerals* (World's Fair Edition). Santa Fe, NM, The New Mexico Printing Company, 1904.

Knight, P. J. "The Flora of the Sangre de Christo Mountains" in *Tectonic Development of the Southern Sangre de Christo Mountains*. Socorro, New Mexico: New Mexico Geological Society, 1990.

Krehbiel, Laura R. *Red River, New Mexico. Your Mountain Playground*. Clayton, New Mexico: Krehbiel, 1939.

Lavender, David. *Bent's Fort*. Lincoln, Neb.: Univ. of Nebraska Press, 1954.

Lavender, David. *The Southwest*. Albuquerque, NM : Univ. of New Mexico Press, 1980.

Lingren, W., L. C. Graton, and C. H. Gordon. "The Ore Deposits of New Mexico". *United States Geological Survey, Professional Paper 68*, Washington, D. C.: U. S. Government Printing Office, 1916.

Moreno Valley Writers Guild. *Lure, Lore, and Legends, A History of Northern New Mexico's Moreno Valley*. Angel Fire, NM: Columbine Books, 1997.

Murphy, Lawrence. *Philmont, a History of New Mexico's Cimarron Country*. Albuquerque, NM: Univ. of New Mexico Press, 1972.

Pearson, Jim Berry. *The Maxwell Land Grant*. Norman, OK: Univ. of Oklahoma Press, 1961.

Pearson, Jim Berry. *The Red River - Twining Area: A New Mexico Mining Story*. Albuquerque, NM: Univ. of New Mexico Press. 1986.

Pettit. "Mineral Resources of Colfax County, Socorro, NM", *New Mexico Bureau of Mines and Mineral Resources, Open File No.15*, 1946.

Ray, Grace E. "Mountain Man" in *New Mexico Magazine*. Albuquerque, October, 1940.

Raymond, Rossiter. "Statistics of Mines and Mining in the States and Territories West of the Rocky Mountains." U.S. Commisioner of Mining Statistics report to Secretary of Treasury, Washington, D. C.: Government Printing Office, 1870.

Ream, Glen O. *Out of New Mexico's Past*. Santa Fe, NM: Sundial Books,1980

Schilling, John H. Mineral "Resources of Taos County, New Mexico, Socorro, NM", New Mexico Bureau of Mines and Mineral Resources, 1982.

Sherman, James E. and Barbara H. Sherman. *Ghost Towns and Mining Camps of New Mexico*. Norman, OK : University of Oklahoma Press, 1975.

Simion, Tillie, edited by Judy Wallner. *Tillie: An American Life*. Roy, New Mexico: Floersheim Printing Co., 1981.

Smith, Toby. *Coal Town. The Life and Times of Dawson, New Mexico*. Santa Fe, New Mexico: Ancient City Press, 1946.

Stanley, F. *The Eagle Nest, New Mexico Story*. Nazareth, Texas, 1973.

Stanley, F. *The Elizabethtown, New Mexico Story*. Dumas, Texas, 1961.

Stanley, F. *The LaBelle, New Mexico Story*. Pantex, Texas, 1962.

BIBLIOGRAPHY

Stanley, F. *The Red River, New Mexico Story*. Nazareth, Texas, 1973.

Walker, Mary Jo. *The F. Stanley Story*. Albuquerque, NM: New Mexico Book League, 1985.

Williams, Jerry L. *New Mexico in Maps*. Albuquerque, NM: Univ. of New Mexico Press, 1986.

Yeager, Ruth. *Red River Community House*, Yeager, 1977.

Zimmer, Stephen. *For Good or Bad. People of the Cimarron Country*. Santa Fe, NM: Sunstone Press, 1999.

Newspapers

La Belle Cresset
Red River Collosal
Red River Miner
Red River Prospector
Red River Ranger
The Red River Rustler
Sangre de Christo Chronicle
Santa Fe New Mexican
Taos El Crepusculo

Historical Society Records

The Red River Historical Society has a large collection of information dealing with Red River history - articles, writings, anecdotes, photos, etc.- which have come from a variety of sources. These records have proven invaluable and are the basis of much that is in this book.

INDEX

A

Ajax Mine 85
All Seasons 184, 202
Allen family 177
Alpine Lodge 159, 161, 163
Alpine Motel 162
Amizette 41, 43, 45, 46, 48
Anchor 66, 68, 71, 72, 82, 86, 95, 110
Annual Enchanted Circle Bike Tour 204
arrastra 97
Arroyo Hondo 46, 48
Aspen Park Guest Ranch 142
Aspencade Arts and Crafts Show 203
Aunt Becky 132, 133, 134, 135
Aztec Mine 52, 95

B

Bainbridge, A. W. (Buzz) 160
Balcomb, Kenneth 116, 117
Baldy Mountain 50, 95
Ball mills 97
Beaubien
    Charles 18, 23, 24, 29, 30, 32
    Luz 29
    Narciso 25, 30, 31, 32, 33, 64
    Paulita 24, 25, 29
Beaubien-Miranda Land Grant 25, 33
Becknell, William 13, 15
Bent
    Charles 18, 20, 22, 30, 31, 32
    Ignacia 23, 31
    William 20, 22
Bent, St. Vrain & Company 21, 22, 23, 29
Bent's Fort 22
Big Chief Trading Post 184
Big Ditch 54, 55, 56, 57, 60, 73
Big Hill 81
Big Oldies Car Show 204
Bittercreek 3, 67, 74, 86, 93, 98, 101
Black Copper 131
Black Copper Creek 74, 88
Black Copper Mine 80, 88, 89, 92
Blanchard, George 194
Bliss, Fanny 195
Bobcat Pass Road 170
Bolton, Audrey 159
Bolton, Stokes 158, 159, 164

Bowser family 173
Bowser, Gary 171
Bowser, Lovilla 171
Brandenburg
    Aileen 126, 151
    Harry 80, 88, 124
    John 125, 126
    John H. 151
    John Jr. 126
    Lottie 125, 126
    Margaret 80
    Rosemary 151
Brandenburg family 186
Brandenburg, John 169, 186, 202
Brandenburg, Johnny 173
Brandenburg, Lottie 178
Brandenburg Park 191
Brandenburg, Rosemary 186, 202
Brandenburgs 114, 151, 152
Bretts Homestead Steakhouse 185
Brunson, Judy 197, 203
Brunson, Roy 184
Buchanan, Don 182, 183
Buchanan family 182
Buchanan, Heather 183
Buchanan, Loveta 182, 183
Bud Fisher family 181
Buffalo Mine 86, 102, 111
Bull of the Woods mine 45
Bunker Hill Mine 87

C

Calhoun, Bernice 173
Calhoun, Beth 175
Calhoun family 173
Calhoun, Glen 173
Calhoun, Glenda 173
Calhoun, Ted 175, 190
Campbell, D.A. 151
Cannard, Joe 131, 132
Caribel Milling and Mining Company 103
Caribel Mine 105, 106, 107, 111, 131
Carson, Josefa 31
Carson, Kit 18, 20, 25, 26, 27, 30, 33, 43
Carson National Forest 5, 129, 130
Catskill 65, 67, 70, 82
Cimarron 35, 82
Cimarron Cutoff 15, 16

Cimarron River 38
Clapper, C.C. 110
Coffelt, Phillip B. 133
Comanche Creek 64, 73
Community House 147, 148, 149
Costilla Estate 64, 98
Costilla watershed 64
Crowe, George (Lee) 103, 105

D

Davis, Fritz 197, 198
Densow, Alyce 198, 200, 201
Densow, Ken 200, 201
Der Markt 169, 175, 203
Dexter's Trading Post 176
Ditch Cabin 54

E

Eagle Nest 62
East Fork 3
Edelweiss 164
Edison Mine 66, 86, 102, 131
Eisenhut 164
Eleanor dredge 61, 62
Elizabethtown
    41, 42, 51, 52, 58, 59, 60, 63, 70, 73, 82, 96
Enchanted Forest 167, 194

F

Fisher family 181
floral life zones 5
Forest Service 130
Fort Union 32, 50, 51
Franklin Placer Company 89
Fraser Mountain 3, 5, 47
Fraser Mountain Copper Company 48
Fraser, William 44, 45, 47, 48
Freehold Land and Emigration Company 64, 65, 74
Friends of the Library 196, 197
Frye, Garnett 171, 173
Frye, Thurline 171
Frye's Melodrama 181
Frye's Old Town 202
Frye's Old Town 172
fur trade 12, 13

G

Gallagher
    Bud 139, 140
    Greta 140
    Opal 139
Gallagher and Guinn Stable 139
Gallagher family 139, 140
Gill, Bill family 180
Gill, James O. 87

Gill, Tom 88
Glen Calhoun Real Estate 175
Goins, Geoff 194
Gold Hill 3, 5, 6, 46
Golden Calf Mine 87, 103
Golden Treasure Mine 87, 103, 111
Goose Creek 3
Grandview Camp 123
Grindstaff, Bill 202
Grindstaff, Maxine 202

H

Hamilton, Walter 119, 120, 185, 202
Hamilton, Winnie 110, 119, 120, 121, 178, 185, 202
Hamiltons 151
Hatton, Ed 93
Helphenstine, Al 45
Hidden Valley 171
Highlander Restaurant 184
Hix, Chuck 194
Hoag, John 199
Hoag, Linda 199
hydraulic mining 52, 53

I

ice harvest 146
Iliff, E. W. 65, 68
Independence Mine 98, 101, 111
Indians
    Jicarilla Apaches 36, 37
    Taos Pueblo Indians 36, 38
    Utes 36, 37
Inferno Mine 85
Iron Flume 55, 56, 57

J

Janney, Joe 197
Jaramillo, Josefa 29
Jayhawk Mine 86, 102, 111
Jayhawk Store 79, 84, 93
Joe Cannard 134
Johnson
    Horace (Cap) 123, 149, 151
    Mary 124, 149
    Will 145
    Dolly 110, 145
Johnson, Dolly 169
Johnson, Will 169
Jones, E.I. 76, 78
Judycki, Drew 194
June Bug Mine 86, 93, 101, 102, 105

K

Kearny, General Stephen 29, 30

L

La Belle
   41, 42, 47, 60, 64, 65, 66, 72, 73, 82, 94, 95, 110
La Belle Cresset 65, 68, 72
Lamb, Mary 184
Lamb, P. W. 190
Lamb, Pat 184
Lambert, Henry 58, 59
land titles 79
Lee, Stephen 25, 30, 33, 64
Lewis
   Jessie 136
   L.S. 136, 148, 149
   Leffy 136
   Lester 138, 190
Lewis, Cliff 185
Lewis family 136, 137, 138
Lewis, L. S. 181
Lewis, Lester 166, 184, 185
Lewis Ranch 136, 137, 139
Lifts West 169
Little Red School House 83, 111, 179, 198
Lynch, Matthew 52, 56, 59

M

Mallette
   George 75, 76, 78
   Julia 76
   Mary Emma 76
   Orrin 75, 76, 77
   Sylvester 75, 76, 78, 94
Mallette Canyon 85
Mallette Creek 3
Mallette Park 191
Mardi Gras in the Mountains 204
Maxwell Land Grant 34, 52
Maxwell Land Grant Company 61, 74
Maxwell, Lucien 18, 28, 32, 33, 37, 52
Maxwell, Luz 33
Maxwell's ranch 35, 38, 58
Melson cabin 118, 121
Melson, Thomas 75
Memphis Mine 86, 93, 99, 101
Mexican land grant system 24
Mexican-American War 29
Middlefork 3
Midnight City
   66, 67, 68, 70, 71, 72, 82, 86, 94, 95, 110
Midnight Mine 66
Miller children 167
Miller family 171
Miller, John 166, 190, 194
Miller, Judy 166, 167, 194
mining 42
mining industry 83
Miranda, Guadalupe 25, 33
Moad, Jarret 75
Moberg, Harry 103

Moly Mine 8, 106, 108, 142, 144
Moly Mine school 179
Moly Mine schoolhouse 107, 109, 110, 120, 138
Molybdenum Corporation of America 107
Monte Vista 158, 171, 175
Monte Vista Lodge 144, 163
Moore, Elizabeth 61
Moore, William 50
Moreno Valley 5, 42, 44, 50, 55, 73, 95
Moreno Water and Mining Company 54
mountain men 12
municipal water system 190
Mutz family 139
Mutz, Henrietta 140, 142
Mutz Hotel 60, 61, 63
Mutz, Johnny 139, 140, 141, 159, 169

N

Neal, T. D. 62
Neptune Mine 99, 101
New Mexico Territory 32

O

Old Pass Road. *See* Red River Pass Road
Old Red River Pass 54, 55
Oldham 74
Oldham assay house 89
Oldham brothers 86, 87, 103, 114, 118, 119, 120
Oldham cabin 87, 91
Oldham water wheel 90
ore crushers 97
Orofino (Big Five) Mine 102, 111

P

Patrick Shop 184
Patrick shop 201
Patrick's Sport Shop 146
Pendley family 184
Phipps 74
Pierce, Jake 203
Pierce, Melville D. 105
Pioneer Canyon 85, 103
Pioneer Creek 3, 74, 75
Pioneer Lodge 145, 169
Pioneer Mining Company 75
Placer Canyon 102
Placer Creek 3, 74, 86
Powder Puff 166, 167, 184, 194
Powder Puff Ski Area 139
Pratt, H.L. 105
Price, Sterling 30
Prunty, Bob 144, 145, 187, 203
Prunty family 144

Q

Querinda 171

R

Raton Pass 13, 15, 16, 22
Rayado Creek 33, 34
Red River
    town of 41, 42, 60, 67, 73, 76, 79, 80, 82, 96
Red River Chamber of Commerce 152
Red River Historical Society 177, 197
Red River Inn 200
Red River Library 177, 195
Red River Miner 198
Red River mines 95
Red River Mining Company 85, 91
Red River Museum 198
Red River Pass 113
Red River Pass Road 116, 117, 118, 122, 169
Red River population 94
Red River Prospector 82
Red River Run 204
Red River schoolhouse 82, 110
Red River Ski Area 193, 194
Red River Ski Resort 159
Red River Valley 41, 54
Red River Women's Club 111, 178, 179
Rio Hondo 42, 43
Riverside 202
Riverside Lodge 177
Romig, Lee 196
Russel's Gift Shop 184

S

Sangre de Christo 2, 3
Sangre de Christo Land Grant 25, 33, 64, 98
Santa Fe Railroad 95
Santa Fe Trail 15, 16, 17
Scarvarda, Louis 99, 101
SEB Motel 159, 160, 161, 165
Shepherd, Kerry 197, 198
Siler, O.B. 131
Silver Spruce Tavern 143
Simeon, Tillie 178
Simion
    Betty 144
    Tillie 142, 143
    Tony 142, 143
    Tony, Jr. 144
Simions 142
Ski Area
    Red River Ski Area 157, 163, 180
Smith, Lily M. 103
Spanish heritage 11
St. James Hotel 59
St. Vrain, Ceran 18, 19, 22, 23, 26, 31, 43
Stamp Mill 90, 92, 97
Starbuck, Fran 166

Starbuck, Gary 166, 167
Stella Mine 85
Stevens, Fremont 82
Stults, David 190
Sundance 146, 199
Sylvester Mallette cabin 144

T

Tall Pine Camp 114, 119, 120, 121
Tall Pine Resort 185
Taos 17
Taos Indians 31
Taos Pueblo 32
Taos Ski Area 50
Taos Uprising 31–33
telephone
    first line 149
Texas Red's 203
Texas Red's Steakhouse 181
The Playhouse 137, 139, 143, 181, 182, 202
The Starr 146, 183, 202
Three Canyon Camp 123
Tompkins, Ann 201, 202
Tompkins, Mel 201
Tony's Bar and Tillie's Cafe 143
tourists 128, 129
Town Hall 192, 193
Treaty of Guadalupe Hidalgo 32
Tweed, Lottie 184
Tweed, Ray 184
Twining 8, 41, 43, 48, 96, 110
Twining, Albert 48

U

U.S. Freehold Land and Emigration Company 98
Upper Valley 158, 170, 175

V

Valley of the Pines 158, 171, 175
Veale, Dr. J. B. 165
Veale, J. B. 194

W

Wagner, Nell 110
Walthall, Dexter 176
Walthall, Frances 176
water wheel 97
Waterbury Watch Company mine 75
Westoby, Ed 75, 85, 107
Wheatcroft, Ed 110, 117
Wheeler Peak 2, 3, 5, 6, 131
Wheeler Village 171
Wild West Melodrama 173
Williams, Don 176
Williams, Frances 176, 177

Williams, Francis 197
Williams Trading Post 176, 202
Willow Creek 50
Woerndle, George 161, 162
Woerndle, Ilse 160, 163
Woerndle, Rudi 161, 162
Woerndle, Toni 158, 160, 163

Y

Yeager, Hal 148
Yeager, Ruth 147, 148, 149
Young, Brigham J. 74, 79, 80, 85, 93, 95
Young, Dorris 178
Young, Gene 123, 152
Young, Harold 197, 202
Young house 81
Young, Jesse 94, 95, 114, 118, 121, 122, 123
Young, Jesse family
    Augusta 186
    Gene 186
    Harold 186
    Jesse 186
    Marie 186
Young, Sara 79, 80
Young's Ranch 114, 152, 185

Z

Zehna, Dan 146